WOODWORKING \
HAND
TOOLS

TOOLS, TECHNIQUES & PROJECTS

EDITORS OF **FINE WOODWORKING**

The Taunton Press

THE TAUNTON PRESS, INC.
63 South Main Street, PO Box 5506
Newtown, CT 06470-5506
E-mail: tp@taunton.com

EDITOR: Christina Glennon
COPY EDITOR: Candace B. Levy
INDEXER: Jay Kreider
JACKET/COVER DESIGN: Guido Caroti
INTERIOR DESIGN: Carol Singer
LAYOUT: Susan Lampe-Wilson

Fine Woodworking® is a trademark of The Taunton Press, Inc., registered in the U.S. Patent and Trademark Office.

The following names/manufacturers appearing in *Woodworking with Hand Tools* are trademarks: 3-in-One®, Auriou™, Bad Axe Tool Works™, Disston®, Eze-Lap™, Forstner®, Gramercy Tools®, iGaging®, Lee Valley Tools®, Lie-Nielsen®, Marples®, Masonite®, Robert Larson Company™, Sharpie®, Stanley®, Starrett®, Trend®, Tried & True™, Veritas®, WD-40®

Library of Congress Cataloging-in-Publication Data

Names: Taunton Press, author.
Title: Woodworking with hand tools : tools, techniques & projects / editors
   of Fine Woodworking.
Other titles: Fine woodworking.
Description: Newtown, CT : Taunton Press, Inc., [2018] | Includes index.
Identifiers: LCCN 2017050132 | ISBN 9781631869396
Subjects: LCSH: Woodwork. | Woodworking tools.
Classification: LCC TT185 .W664 2018 | DDC 684/.082--dc23
LC record available at https://lccn.loc.gov/2017050132

Printed in the United States of America
10 9 8 7 6 5 4 3 2 1

ABOUT YOUR SAFETY: Working wood is inherently dangerous. Using hand or power tools improperly or ignoring safety practices can lead to permanent injury or even death. Don't try to perform operations you learn about here (or elsewhere) unless you're certain they are safe for you. If something about an operation doesn't feel right, don't do it. Look for another way. We want you to enjoy the craft, so please keep safety foremost in your mind whenever you're in the shop.

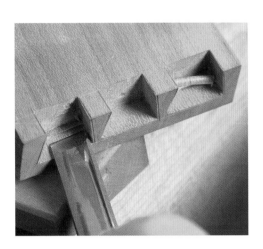

ACKNOWLEDGMENTS

Special thanks to the authors, editors, art directors, copy editors, and other staff members of *Fine Woodworking* who contributed to the development of the chapters in this book.

Contents

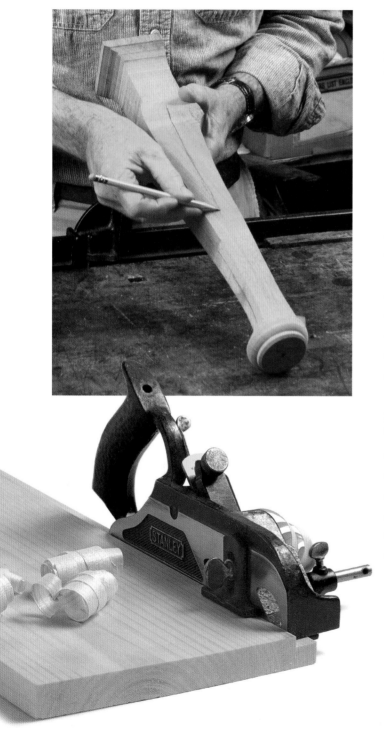

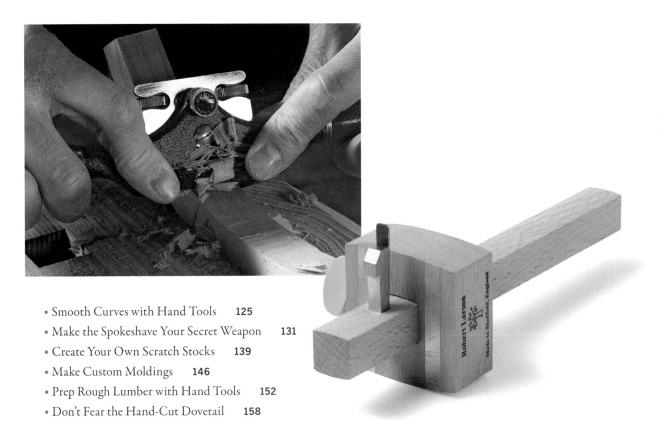

PART THREE

Projects

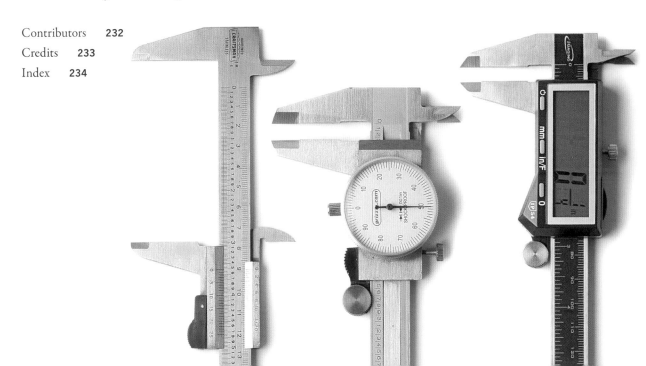

Introduction

There's been an emphatic upsurge in hand-tool woodworking in recent years, and it's easy to understand why. Working wood with hand tools can be a pure pleasure: It's an activity that combines freehand shaping with precision joinery and enjoyable exertion with self-expression. And all of that while you explore a material that is aesthetically beguiling and aromatic to boot. Some woodworkers have put their routers, tablesaws, and biscuit machines aside in favor of planes, chisels, and hand saws; others continue to rely on their machines and power tools but have shifted the balance in their shops toward tools that work fine when unplugged.

While hand-tool woodworking can be a delight, getting good at it takes time and effort and, for many, much trial and error. The only shortcut to mastery that I know of is a good teacher. Or seventeen. If you are drawn toward hand-tool woodworking—or are already immersed in it—you'll find this book an unparalleled resource. It brings together contributions by masters of the craft who are also superb instructors. In pieces originally published in the pages of *Fine Woodworking* magazine, these expert makers invite you to the bench as they explain the fundamentals and fine points of working with hand tools.

The first third of the book explores the tools themselves, with investigations of everything from scrapers and saws, cutting gauges and combination squares, to joinery planes and Japanese chisels, shoulder planes and skew chisels. The second third presents hand tool techniques, moving from explanations of how to sharpen up fundamental skills like chiseling, sawing, and planing, through to making your own moldings with a scratch stock and smoothing curves with a spokeshave, and ending with an outstanding treatise on the handcut dovetail. Finally, the third part provides complete project instructions for making a selection of hand tools by hand.

To take advantage of all this expertise, simply turn the page. By hand.

—Jonathan Binzen,
Deputy Editor, *Fine Woodworking*

PART ONE
TOOLS

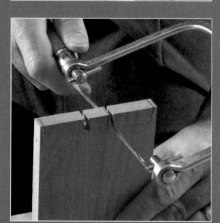

Essential Hand-Tool Kit

DAN FAIA

I've done all sorts of woodworking in my career, but hand tools have always played a large role. I cannot do my best work without them.

Whether working in the big shop at North Bennet Street School, where I teach, using an equal balance of power and hand, or working in my home shop almost exclusively at the bench, my set of essential hand tools is surprisingly similar.

While I was designing a compact tool rack recently, I gave serious thought to just which tools I rely on, the ones I reach for on a regular basis. Granted, I am a period furniture maker by trade, and I probably work with more curves and carving than the average woodworker. So you might be able to get away without a couple of the items on my list. And some woodworkers will want to add a block plane, for trimming small surfaces and making shaping cuts. I prefer to handle these tasks with the other tools in my kit, but the block plane can be very helpful.

Layout

Layout tools are the foundation for accurate work, helping me create precise joinery, angles, and curves. They also serve as important references for squareness and flatness.

The **combination square** is the primary benchmark in the shop. A machinist-quality model is accurate and easy to read. Its many tasks include measuring workpieces,

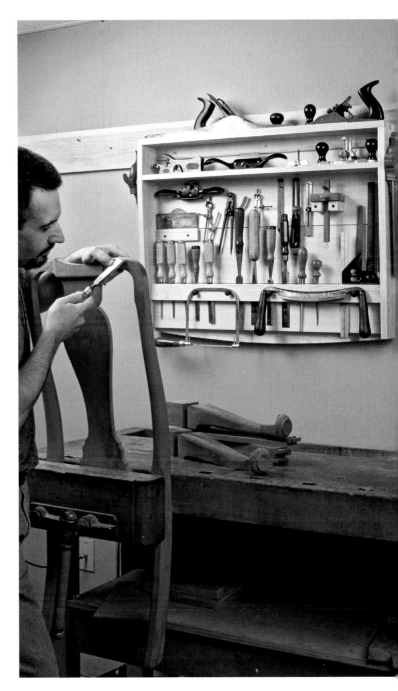

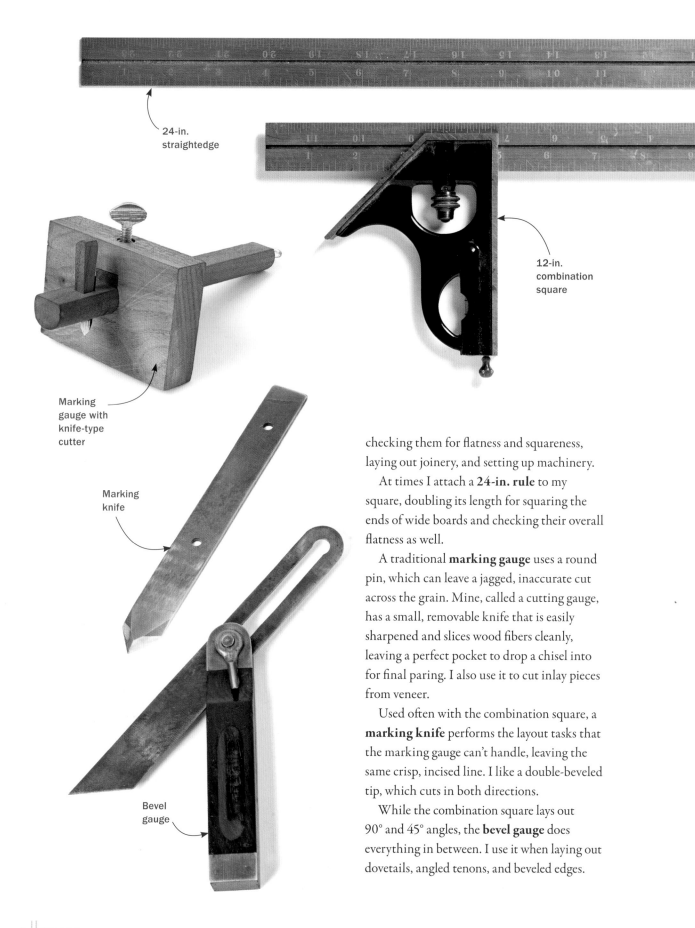

24-in. straightedge

12-in. combination square

Marking gauge with knife-type cutter

Marking knife

Bevel gauge

checking them for flatness and squareness, laying out joinery, and setting up machinery.

At times I attach a **24-in. rule** to my square, doubling its length for squaring the ends of wide boards and checking their overall flatness as well.

A traditional **marking gauge** uses a round pin, which can leave a jagged, inaccurate cut across the grain. Mine, called a cutting gauge, has a small, removable knife that is easily sharpened and slices wood fibers cleanly, leaving a perfect pocket to drop a chisel into for final paring. I also use it to cut inlay pieces from veneer.

Used often with the combination square, a **marking knife** performs the layout tasks that the marking gauge can't handle, leaving the same crisp, incised line. I like a double-beveled tip, which cuts in both directions.

While the combination square lays out 90° and 45° angles, the **bevel gauge** does everything in between. I use it when laying out dovetails, angled tenons, and beveled edges.

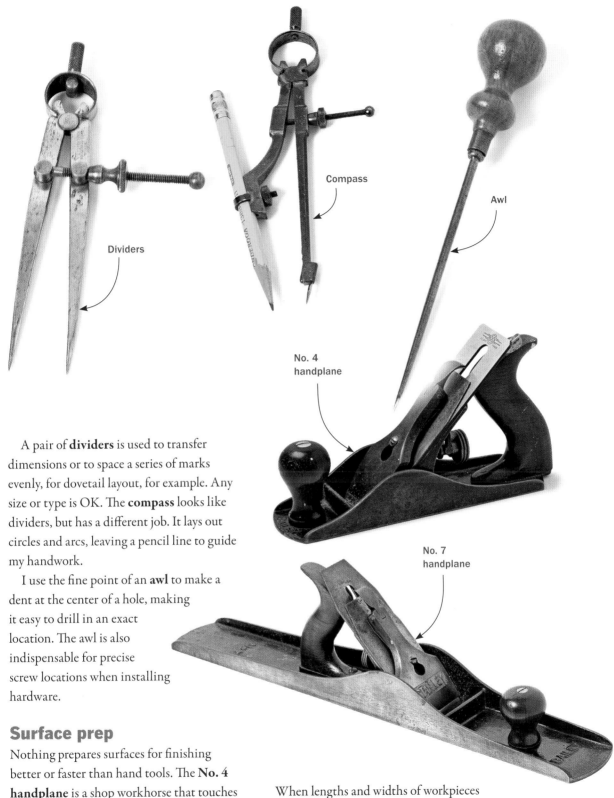

Dividers

Compass

Awl

No. 4
handplane

No. 7
handplane

A pair of **dividers** is used to transfer dimensions or to space a series of marks evenly, for dovetail layout, for example. Any size or type is OK. The **compass** looks like dividers, but has a different job. It lays out circles and arcs, leaving a pencil line to guide my handwork.

I use the fine point of an **awl** to make a dent at the center of a hole, making it easy to drill in an exact location. The awl is also indispensable for precise screw locations when installing hardware.

Surface prep

Nothing prepares surfaces for finishing better or faster than hand tools. The **No. 4 handplane** is a shop workhorse that touches almost every surface. Unlike sandpaper, the plane maintains a flat surface and leaves a pristine cut, and does it quickly. I also like its mass and momentum for squaring and beveling edges, and shaping convex surfaces.

When lengths and widths of workpieces outmatch the No. 4, the **No. 7** gets the job done. The long sole creates flawless edge joints on long pieces and is great for truing doors and frames. This big plane is ideal for flattening large panels quickly.

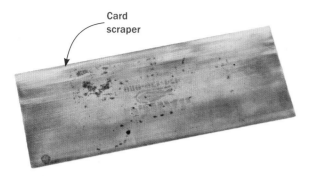

Card scraper

A **cabinet scraper**, based on the Stanley® No. 80, scrapes in a more systematic way than the humble card scraper, making it easier to maintain a flat surface. It is not an everyday player in the kit, but it does an incredible job on large surfaces with difficult grain.

To sharpen scrapers of all kinds, you need a **burnisher**. They come in many shapes: round, triangular, and teardrop. I prefer the round, tapered type, which has a pointed tip that I use to realign the burr.

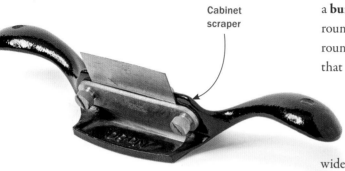

Cabinet scraper

Joinery

Forming joinery is job one for the following list of tools, which make a wide variety of helpful cuts.

To make straight joinery cuts, you need two saws. The **dovetail saw** cuts cleanly and efficiently with the grain. I use it mostly to cut dovetails and tenon cheeks. The **carcase saw** handles bigger jobs that require more cutting length and depth. I use it to cut tenon shoulders and dadoes, and also to cut parts to length, mitered or square.

Not as precise as the first two saws, the **coping saw** is a highly underrated tool. It is great for removing rough material when cutting joints, but it's also useful for cutting curves. A good-quality blade makes all the difference. I recommend Stanley blades, with

Burnisher

For ornery grain, when the handplanes are leaving too much tearout, the **card scraper** steps in, reducing the amount of sanding required. It is also invaluable for flushing veneers and inlay without damaging the surrounding surface. I use curved card scrapers (called gooseneck scrapers) to smooth moldings and other curves.

Dovetail saw

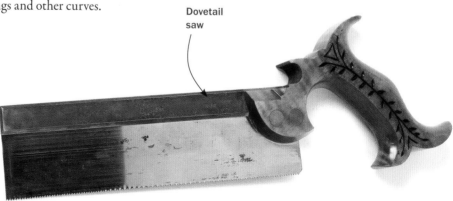

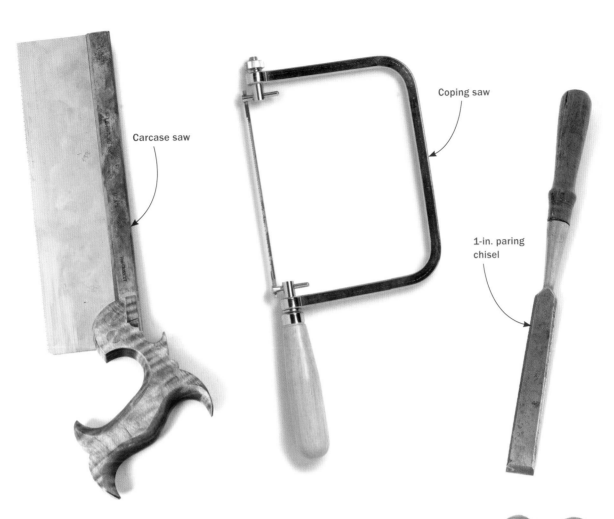

Carcase saw

Coping saw

1-in. paring chisel

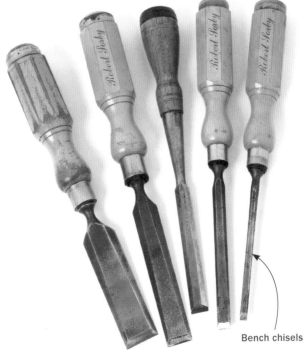

15 tpi (teeth per inch). They work well on both hardwoods and softwoods.

A **set of five chisels** (¼ in., ⅜ in., ½ in., ¾ in., and 1 in.) is adequate for most tasks in the shop, from chopping and paring joinery to shaping wood. By far, the 1-in. chisel is the most used in my set. Round out your basic chisel kit with a 1-in. paring chisel. Its longer, thinner blade fits into tight quarters and reaches far beyond a standard chisel. I use it to trim tenon cheeks as well as for all sorts of shaping cuts, from curves to chamfers.

Fitting joinery is one of the most important and fundamental tasks in

Bench chisels

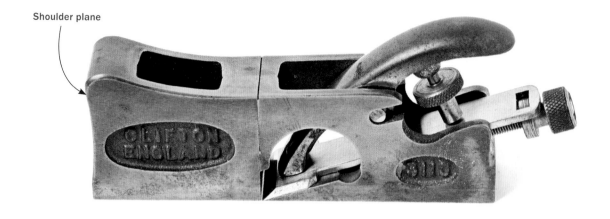

Shoulder plane

furniture making. A **shoulder plane**, designed to pare surfaces precisely all the way into a corner, brings a wonderful level of precision to this task, making it easy to fit tenons, rabbets, and much more. It will become a go-to tool in your kit.

The **router plane** is a very versatile tool. Its sole rests on the surface of the work, with a cutter hanging down to produce a surface parallel to the top one. It's great for cutting pockets for inlay, refining the bottoms of dadoes, and relieving the background of a carving. I use a large model for larger areas, and a small model with a ⅛-in.-wide cutter. The small plane can ride on narrower surfaces for more delicate inlay and hardware jobs.

Shaping

The following tools shape wood in various ways, from rough to refined. If your work doesn't involve many 3-D curves, you can probably get away without the drawknife and rasp.

The **drawknife** is good for more than shaping green wood, its traditional job. It makes quick work of bevels, roughing them out before a shave or plane takes over. And it's great for sculpting 3-D surfaces such as a cabriole leg.

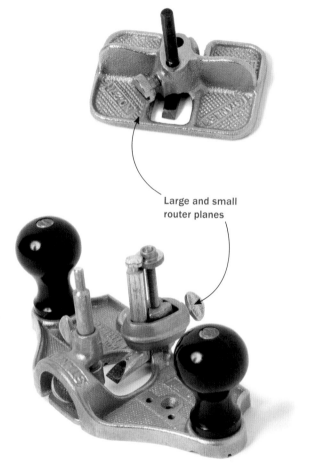

Large and small router planes

A standard metal-bodied **spokeshave** is a planing tool with a short, flat sole, ideal for smoothing and refining the curved cuts of a bandsaw, coping saw, or drawknife.

The cabinetmaker's **rasp** is used like a drawknife or spokeshave to form and refine

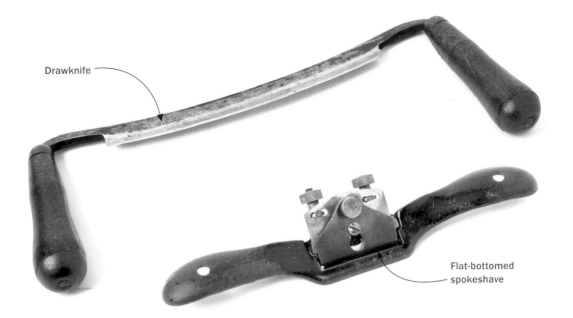

Drawknife

Flat-bottomed
spokeshave

curves of any shape, but its abrading cut makes it better on difficult grain. Use a **half-round file** to refine the surface left by the rasp, or simply to shape a surface where the rasp would be too aggressive. I like the double-cut pattern.

A second file, the **mill file**, is a must-have for the inevitable metalwork in a woodworking shop, like tuning up hand tools and modifying hardware. It also leaves a smooth surface on wood.

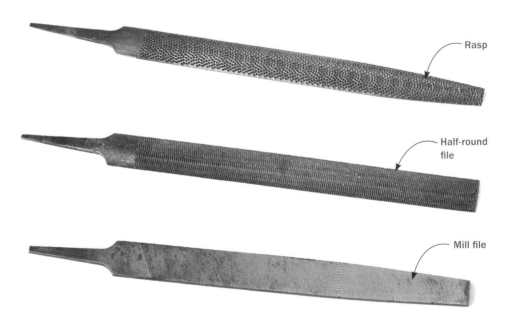

Rasp

Half-round
file

Mill file

Combo Squares: The Basics and Beyond

TIMOTHY ROUSSEAU

Every fall, a new group of students begins the 12-week furniture-making program at the Center for Furniture Craftsmanship in Maine, where I teach. They spend the first few weeks learning to tune and use essential hand tools like chisels, planes, and saws. They also learn about layout tools, and it doesn't take them long to understand why one layout tool, the combination square, is perhaps the most useful of all. I know I couldn't work without at least one close at hand.

Many woodworkers understand the fundamental uses for combination squares, such as laying out joinery or checking to see if the corner of a case is square. But they're good for so much more. I find them invaluable for diagnosing why a joint won't come together or close up without gaps, and for checking the joint's accuracy after it is assembled. Here, I'll help you master this fundamental tool. Once you do, the combination square will help you do better work.

Checking for square. Because 90° cuts are so common and critical in furniture making, you'll use the combination square most often to verify the accuracy of corners and joinery. The 12-in. square works best across the end grain as shown here. Hold the square's body in your dominant hand and press the head against the board's edge. Slide the blade down until it touches the end grain. If you see light coming through, the cut is not square.

On the edge. The technique used for end grain works here, too, but a 4-in. square is better because it's easier to balance on the narrow edge.

Joints need checking, too. For inside corners, you'll need to push the blade into the body and lock it in place. This setup can be used to check dry-assembled cases and miter joints to determine if they're square.

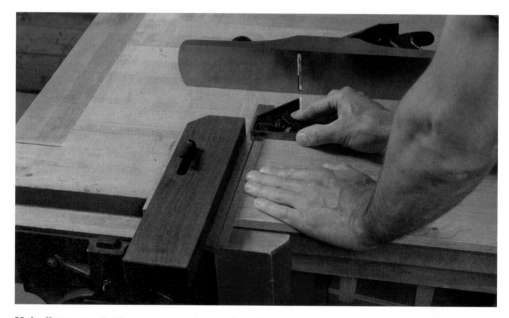

Make jigs accurate. To square up a shooting board's fence, register the head against the runway and the blade against the jig's fence.

Start with a 6-in. square

Combination squares come in a variety of sizes, but the most useful sizes for furniture making are the 4-in., 6-in., and 12-in. models. Of the three, I use my 6-in. square the most. It's small enough to fit into joints like mortises and between dovetails, but it's big enough for machinery setup. It's also easy to control when laying out joints. However, I do use the 12-in. square often, and I keep a 4-in. square in my apron pocket to help fit dovetails and to quickly check edges for square. If you're just starting out, get the 6-in. combination square first, followed by the 12-in. model. The 4-in. square can wait.

How to hold the square. When marking across a narrow edge, pinch the square's head against the board, using three fingers on the head and your thumb on the board. Use your index finger to hold down the blade (left). The grasp is nearly the same when marking across the face of a board. However, because your thumb can't reach the far edge, use it to help hold down the blade (right).

Two heads are better. Rousseau puts two heads on a 24-in. blade to lay out joinery on wide panels. With this setup, it's a snap to lay out identical joinery at different locations, such as dadoes for shelves in case sides.

Working with one head. This is more accurate than using a ruler to locate a joint, because the head gives you positive registration off the end grain and is repeatable from one board to the next.

Miter joints on the edge. The angled fence on a small 4-in. or 6-in. combination square is easier to manage when laying out a miter on the edge of a board, say, for a mitered dovetail. The grip is the same as it is for square layout.

On the face. Use the angled fence of a larger 12-in. square to mark wide miters like those for a picture frame. Use your thumb and index finger to offset the head's weight.

Accurate mortise and tenon. The combination square can be used to dial in the fit of a test joint, or as a diagnostic tool to discover why a joint doesn't go together the way it should. To measure the mortise depth, loosen the blade, place the head on the stile, and slide the blade down until it bottoms out in the mortise. Lock the blade.

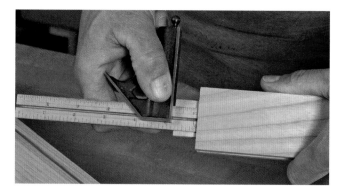

Compare it to tenon's cheeks. If the head sits on the end grain while the blade hits the shoulder, the tenon is just right.

Keep it centered. Set the blade against one cheek, then check from the other side.

The rule etched into the blade of a combination square is available in a dizzying array of scales, but almost all of them are meant for machinists and other metal workers. As a woodworker, you should get the "4R grad" rule, which has ⅛-in. and 1/16-in. increments on one side and 1/32-in. and 1/64-in. increments on the other.

If you're in the mood to lavish yourself with a specialized tool, get a combination square with a 24-in. blade. With a second head attached, it becomes a great layout tool for case joinery.

As for what brand to buy, I've had good luck with Starrett® combination squares, and I recommend them to my students.

A good grip improves accuracy

The head of a combination square is much heavier than the blade. Because the head hangs off the side of the board during layout, it can be tricky to keep the square steady, especially since you hold it with your non-dominant hand. Not steadying the head can lead to bad layout.

Dialing in dovetails. The combination square is a handy aid from beginning to end. You can use it to help with layout, to check for high spots on shoulders, and for cheeks that bulge. The 1-in.-wide blade of a 12-in. combo square can be used to set a bevel gauge to common dovetail angles such as 1:6 and 1:8. Extend the blade so its length matches the slope number (6 in. for 1:6). Then mark on both sides of the ruler at the board's edge, along the sides, and the top edge (1). Use the square's blade to draw a line from the bottom corner on one side to the top corner on the other side (2). Place the bevel gauge's body against the board's edge and angle the blade to match the sloping line (3). Now you're ready to lay out some dovetails.

Keep the shoulders square. Press the head against the tail board's surface and lower the blade. Run it back and forth to find high spots.

The solution is to use your pinky and the two fingers next to it to press the head against the edge of the board. If the board is narrow enough, reach across it with your thumb and pinch the board between your thumb and the square's head. Press down on the blade with your index finger. This grip keeps the square tight against the board with the blade flat on the workpiece, which allows you to use your other hand to get a precise mark with a pencil or knife. If the board is too wide to pinch, then use your thumb and index finger to press down on the blade.

You're now ready to put the combination square to use for laying out joints and checking their accuracy.

How flat is the webbing? Extend the blade to match the length of the tails. With the head on the pin board, slide it through the socket to determine where to pare.

Check the cheeks, too. With the head on the end grain, you can check them for plumb. You also can check the shoulder this way.

Every Woodworker Needs a Cutting Gauge

TIMOTHY ROUSSEAU

Tight joinery begins with crisp, accurate layout. This is why a scribed or cut line is better than a pencil line for most layout work. A knife and square can be used for most (if not all) layout jobs, but I find that a gauge is often more efficient and accurate. The three most commonly used in woodworking are the marking gauge, the mortise gauge, and the cutting gauge. Marking and mortise gauges use a pointed pin to scribe lines with the grain, while a cutting gauge has a knifelike blade that slices fibers across the grain.

All three are necessary if you cut joinery by hand, particularly the mortise-and-tenon.

However, if you use a powered apprentice to cut mortises and tenons, then the marking and mortise gauges won't get much use. The cutting gauge, however, is an indispensable tool for furniture making regardless of which tools you use to cut joinery. It's perfect for marking dovetail and tenon shoulders, and can be used to sever fibers and minimize tearout before making a crossgrain cut with a tablesaw or router.

There are two types of cutting gauges. Wheel gauges have a steel beam with a round cutter at the end. The fence is usually round, too. These work fine, but I prefer the traditional-style cutting gauge with a

Quick tune-up for sharper layout. Out of the box, the blade on most cutting gauges is dull and pointed, so it tears out fibers when cutting across the grain (above). However, after refining and sharpening the tip (see p. 22), the same gauge cuts a clean, accurate line.

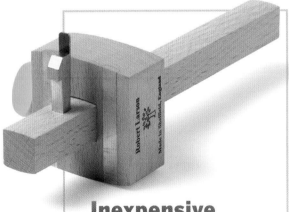

Inexpensive Gauge Gets the Job Done

There are many traditional-style cutting gauges on the market. Of these, Rousseau prefers the Robert Larson Company™ cutting gauge (model #605-1100, www. circlesaw.com). For around $20 and some time spent on a tune-up, he says it can't be beat.

Tune up the fence. A cutting gauge works best when the fence glides smoothly along the edge of the workpiece and the blade cuts parallel to the fence.

The beam and fence should be square. If the beam does not move smoothly through the mortise in the fence, file the mortise.

Smooth the fence face. For accuracy, the brass wear strips should be flush with the fence. If they're not, sand the fence on a flat surface (left), working from 80 grit to 220 grit, until the strips are level (above).

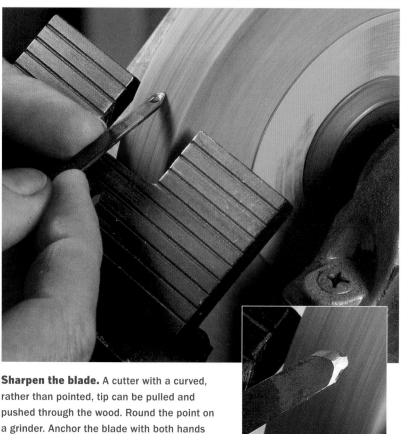

Sharpen the blade. A cutter with a curved, rather than pointed, tip can be pulled and pushed through the wood. Round the point on a grinder. Anchor the blade with both hands and then rotate to create the thumbnail profile (above). The cutting edge should have a slightly rounded tip (right).

wooden beam and fence. The cutter is often a spear-point knife that is held in the beam by a wedge. Because they have a wider fence, I find these gauges track the edge of the board more easily than wheel gauges. However, before you put one to use, it's a good idea to give it a quick tune-up. It's not hard, and I'll show you what to do.

Tweak the fence and cutter

Start with the fence, which must be flat (check it with a 12-in. rule) so that it glides smoothly along the workpiece. Any hiccup caused by the fence is transferred to the cutter, leaving a hiccup in your layout line, too. The result? Joints that aren't as tight as they could be.

Check that the beam is square to the fence. If it's not, use a chisel to pare the wall of the mortise square, then glue a thin shim to the pared wall so that the beam slides smoothly

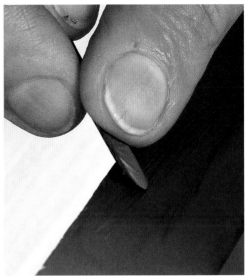

Hone the back and bevel. Start with the back, using the edge of a polishing stone (left). Then polish the bevel (above). Don't worry if the bevel has facets. Only the cutting edge matters.

in the mortise. If the beam is square, slide it back and forth in the mortise. If it is difficult to move, file the mortise until the beam slides smoothly. If the beam moves so easily that it's hard to set and lock it in place, glue in a thin shim. Next, sand the business side of the fence on a flat surface (especially important if there are brass wear strips embedded in the face).

Now move on to the cutter. Like any cutting tool, it must be sharp to perform at its best. I prefer the bevel to have a rounded tip, rather than a pointy one, because it can be pushed and pulled. I round the tip with a slow-speed grinder. I then hone the back and bevel on the edge of a polishing stone. Admittedly, it takes some practice to hone a curved bevel, but it doesn't have to be pretty, just sharp.

When the cutter is sharp, put it back in the beam with the bevel facing the fence.

This pulls the fence against the workpiece during use and also puts the bevel on the waste side of the cut for 99% of joinery layout. The cutter should stick out ³⁄₁₆ in. below the beam. Slide the beam back into the fence, and the cutting gauge is ready to use. Hold it between two fingers and apply sideward pressure against the fence to keep the gauge snug on the workpiece. Take a light cut, and you'll have precise layout lines, the first step toward tight joints.

Machinist's Calipers

TIMOTHY ROUSSEAU

Machinist's calipers may seem like a strange object to find in a woodshop, but when you need to measure something very accurately there isn't a better tool for the job. Consider joinery. For a strong glue bond, a joint should be snug enough that the pieces won't fall apart from gravity alone, but not so tight that they need to be pounded together. That's a small margin of error, and a few thousandths of an inch can make a big difference.

Having a tool that will tell you exactly how big a tenon or mortise is takes away the guesswork as you sneak up on the perfect fit.

The same goes for dadoes, rabbets, and many other joints. You can also use calipers for machine setups of all kinds, so you can nail the fit on the first try.

Dial or digital, take your pick

There are three types of machinist's calipers. Vernier calipers, with their simple sliding scale and fractional markings, are bombproof but less precise than other types. That's because they are hard to read closely, especially if your eyesight is not 100%.

Dial calipers are very precise but vulnerable to breaking if dropped, especially

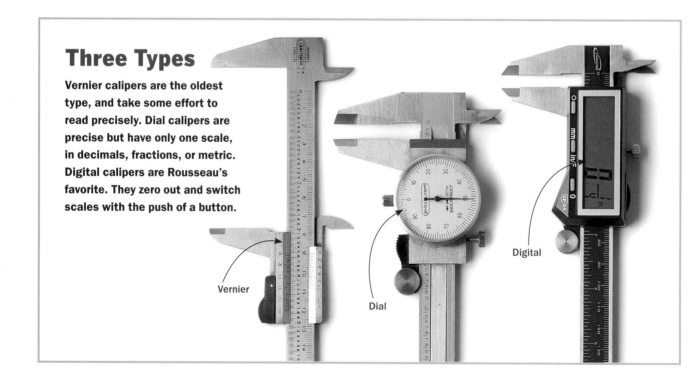

Three Types

Vernier calipers are the oldest type, and take some effort to read precisely. Dial calipers are precise but have only one scale, in decimals, fractions, or metric. Digital calipers are Rousseau's favorite. They zero out and switch scales with the push of a button.

Vernier

Dial

Digital

1

Four ways to measure. A mortise-and-tenon joint shows how calipers can provide precise information to achieve perfect results. Use the outside jaws to measure the thickness of a part such as a tenon, so you know how much more you have to trim off.

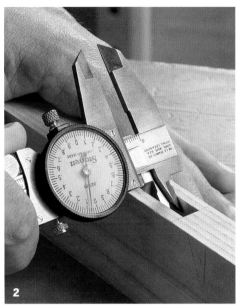

2

Inside for width. Use the inside jaws to find out exactly how wide a mortise is before cutting the tenon. They are also great for positioning a jig on a workpiece and dozens of other tasks.

3

Square and steady. The step on the back of the sliding jaw is often overlooked. It registers squarely against the edge of a workpiece while the end of the tool is used for measuring.

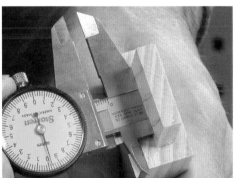

4

Measure or mark. The step lets you use the end of the jaws as a depth stop of sorts, for measuring distances (top). You can also slide the tool along an edge for marking and scribing (above).

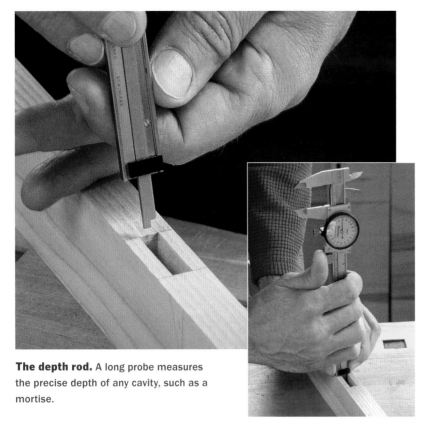

The depth rod. A long probe measures the precise depth of any cavity, such as a mortise.

Add magnets and make machines digital. Use these standoff magnets from Lee Valley Tools® (www.leevalley.com) to attach calipers to a metal surface, and then use the depth rod to make precise adjustments to fences, jigs, and more.

if you buy a cheap one. They also take a moment to read accurately.

My favorite type of calipers is digital. The beauty of digital is instant readability and the ability to switch scales. Most will display thousandths of an inch, fractions of an inch, and metric. I find fractions pretty useless on calipers, but I often switch to metric to make math easier. The model I recommend to my students is the 6-in. electronic digital calipers from iGaging®.

How to take a measurement

Calipers can make a precise measurement in four ways. Most people know about the first three. At the business end you'll find two pairs of jaws that can grab the outside of a workpiece or the inside of a cavity or hole of some kind. When using these jaws, you have to make sure you are not skewing them and getting a false reading. It helps to take a couple of measurements to be sure.

At the far end of the tool you'll find a probe, which moves when the jaws move and measures the depths of holes and mortises. Here, I make sure the body of the tool is touching the surface squarely and then I plunge the probe. Again, I take a couple of readings to make sure I'm getting an accurate one.

A fourth and lesser-known technique is to use the step between the two jaws, on the back of the tool, to measure the distance from an edge. All types of calipers have it. The probe can do a similar measurement, but the advantage of the jaw step is that it registers squarely, without wobbling. With the step riding the edge of a workpiece you can also use the caliper as a layout tool, the way you would use a combination square, but with 0.001-in. precision.

There is a lock knob on top of the jaws, which is helpful when you are working to a specific dimension and you don't want the

Perfect dado joints. Whether fitting a dado to plywood or planing a solid shelf to fit, calipers speed up the process. Use the inside jaws to find the precise width of any dado. For an accurate reading, lay down the calipers as flat as possible, so the jaws sit squarely in the opening.

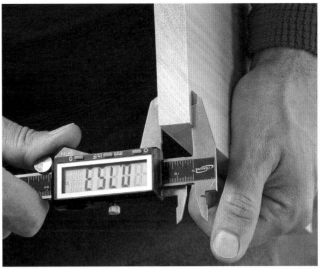

Check your stock. As you plane down your stock to fit, take measurements to see how close you are.

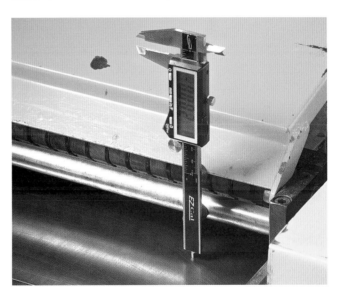

Use the magnet trick. Attach the calipers to your planer with magnets, so you can adjust the bed precisely for the final pass.

setting on the caliper to change. And the dial (both digital and analog) can also be zeroed out in any jaw position.

Perfect mortises and tenons

When making mortise-and-tenon joints with power tools, calipers are a real star. After the mortises are cut, calipers tell you exactly how big they are. You might think that the mortise will be the same size as your router or mortising bit, but runout in the router or problems with a jig or machine setup could change that dimension. By measuring the actual mortise, you can make tenons to fit.

If you prefer cutting joinery entirely by hand, calipers are just as indispensable, checking that the walls of a mortise are parallel to each other and to the outside of the workpiece. Once you have the mortise true and straight, the calipers will tell you if the tenon is staying even in thickness as you cut, and help you dial in the fit.

Precise machine setups, too

Calipers are also indispensable for machine setups, for example when running stock through the planer until it fits perfectly into a dado. I use the inside calipers to take a measurement of the dado and then use the outside ones to sneak up on the right thickness.

When I get close, I actually stick the calipers onto the planer using a set of

Nailed. After the final pass on the planer, the shelf fits its dado perfectly.

standoff magnetic tool holders from Lee Valley Tools. This setup lets me gauge the exact amount I am moving the cutterhead. I just love getting a perfect fit on my second pass, simply by measuring. It saves a bunch of time over guessing.

When going in the other direction—fitting a dado to plywood, for example—I use the calipers to micro-adjust the dado stack for a perfect fit. First I assemble a dado stack that is close, but just under, my shelf size and run a test piece. Then I measure the shelf again, and the dado, and hunt through the shim set with the calipers to find exactly what I need to add to the stack.

Stronger screw connections

Another great task for calipers is sizing the holes for screws. It is very important for the screw to pass freely through the top piece being attached. This is called a clearance hole. The lower piece of wood gets a pilot hole, which is smaller, letting the threads grab the wood firmly without splitting it.

Put simply, calipers are an information-gathering tool—maybe the best one in the shop. And better information leads to better accuracy.

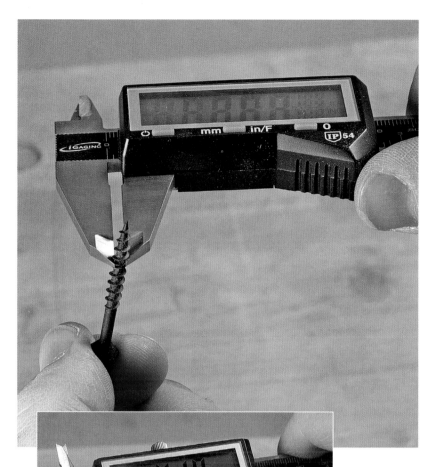

Better Screw Joints

If you drill a precise pilot hole in the bottom piece, plus a slightly larger clearance hole in the top piece, you can get surprising strength from a screw. Calipers measure the screw and help you pick the right drill bits.

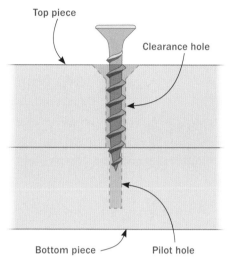

Top piece

Clearance hole

Bottom piece — Pilot hole

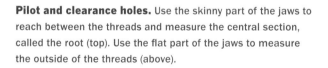

Pilot and clearance holes. Use the skinny part of the jaws to reach between the threads and measure the central section, called the root (top). Use the flat part of the jaws to measure the outside of the threads (above).

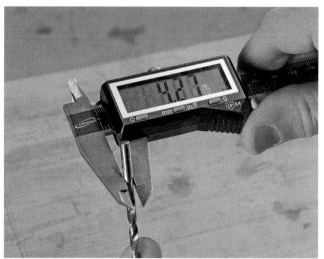

Dial in the bits. Fractional drill sizes can be confusing. Keep it simple by using the decimal scale to pick the right bit.

Mastering the Card Scraper

MATTHEW TEAGUE

O f all the tools in my shop, my favorite is the basic card scraper. It's nothing more than a thin piece of steel that costs a few dollars, but it greatly reduces my least favorite part of woodworking: sanding.

The scraper cleans up tool and milling marks, levels glue-ups, and smooths surfaces.

It removes material as efficiently as sandpaper but doesn't leave scratches in its wake. A scraper is easier to control than a handplane and can surface tricky grain where even a well-tuned plane does more harm than good.

Tuning a card scraper is relatively easy using only a mill file, sandpaper, and

Remove millmarks. A scraper is ideal for cleaning up light tearout and marks from jointers, planers, and handplanes.

Clean glue. Dried squeeze-out comes off easily. Avoid an aggressive cut, which can dish the glueline.

Trim edging. The cut is adjustable enough to trim solid edging flush and avoid damaging the plywood veneer.

Work tricky grain. The scraper works lightly, taking clean shavings despite treacherous changes in grain direction on this walnut-burl board.

a screwdriver. Using a card scraper takes practice, but only a little. In a very short time, you'll be able to cut continuous shavings akin to those you get with a handplane.

Tune-up starts with a mill file

New scrapers need a tune-up, and you'll have to repeat it from time to time, but the good news is that the process only takes three or four minutes.

First, file the long edges flat and square to the faces of the scraper. You can clamp the scraper in a vise and work the edge freehand with a standard mill file, or you can lay the file flat on the bench and work the scraper across it. Take full-length strokes until you feel and hear the file cut continuously.

Next, flatten the scraper's faces. Use a flat sharpening stone or 180-grit wet-or-dry sandpaper attached to a flat surface. Don't work the entire face, just the leading ½ in. or so. Use all eight fingers to apply even pressure, and work until you see a smooth surface with fresh steel exposed all the way to the edge. Then move to 320-grit paper to achieve a cleaner surface. If I'm trying to achieve a very fine, finish cut, I sometimes move on to 400 grit or even 600 grit.

These filing and flattening steps build up a "wire edge" of thin and brittle waste material that must be removed. To do this, hold the face of the scraper at 90° to the stone or sandpaper and work the edge using light pressure. It's easier to maintain the 90° angle if you skew the scraper. After a few strokes,

Filing and Honing

Before you can form consistent burrs at the edges, it is crucial that the edge and sides are smooth and meet at 90°.

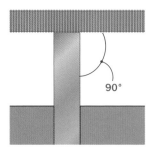

Sharpening starts with a file. Secure the scraper in a vise and use a mill file to remove hardened steel and square the edge. Be sure to keep the file at a 90° angle to the faces of the scraper.

Next hone the faces. Work the scraper back and forth on a sharpening stone or sandpaper set on a flat surface. Use eight fingers to apply even pressure (left). A mirror finish isn't crucial, but a smoother surface (above) yields a more uniform burr.

Remove the wire edge. A few light strokes on edge should accomplish this. Skewing the scraper to the direction of cut helps keep it square to the sanding surface. This also hones the edge, removing any rough file marks.

the wire edge should fall off. If not, give the faces of the scraper a few passes across the sandpaper.

Draw and turn the burr

To create a tough burr for cutting wood, you need a burnisher—a rod of highly polished steel that is harder than the soft steel in the scraper. I've owned several commercially made burnishers over the years and they all worked fine. My favorite now is an old screwdriver.

Creating a burr begins with the scraper flat on the edge of the bench. Hold the burnisher flat against the face while pushing it away from you for several strokes along the length of the edge. Concentrate downward pressure on the cutting edge to draw out the burr. Some woodworkers like to angle the burnisher down on the edge, but this angle should be very slight, only a degree or so. Work until you feel a slight burr when you carefully touch the edge with your fingertip. Draw the burr along each of the scraper's four long edges.

Now clamp the scraper upright in a bench vise with the edge to be burnished parallel to the benchtop. You can turn the burr with the burnisher held freehand or, to ensure a consistent angle, let the handle of the burnisher ride on the benchtop during each stroke. Following this second approach means that adjusting the scraper's height

Raising a Burr

Burnishing each edge forces the metal into a hook shape, creating a cutting burr.

Draw the burr. Apply firm downward pressure with the burnishing rod at the scraper's edge. Take several strokes, always pushing away from you. Skew the burnisher to help force material past the edge of the scraper.

Turn the burr. Use a piece of scrap as a reference to set the scraper's edge at a consistent height. Then ride the burnisher's handle along the bench to maintain a consistent angle and make several firm pushing strokes away from you.

Drawing the burnishing rod over the flat face at a very slight angle extends the corner of the edge out into a ridge.

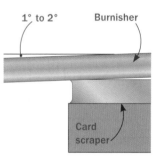

1° to 2°   Burnisher

Card scraper

Use the burnisher at an angle of 1° to 15° to flatten this ridge and create a hook-shaped cutting burr. A steeper angle yields a more aggressive cut.

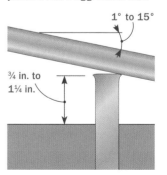

1° to 15°

¾ in. to 1¼ in.

TIP Create an inexpensive heat shield. A flat refrigerator magnet helps protect your thumbs from the heat generated in use.

Two thumbs down. Grasp the scraper with your fingers wrapped around each side and your thumbs together on the back, near the bottom edge. Push forward with your thumbs, applying enough pressure to create a slight bow. The more pronounced the bow, the more aggressive the cut.

in the vise will alter the burnishing angle and, as a result, the cutting angle of the finished burr. The steeper the angle, the more aggressive the cut, but any angle between 1° and 15° works well.

Turning the burr should take only two or three passes. Once you feel a turned burr along the entire edge, test the cut. If you're making only dust, burnish some more. Once you're making shavings with both sides, you're ready to start scraping.

Two ways to take a shaving

A scraper can either be pushed or pulled. I usually push the scraper to make aggressive, slightly concave cuts when removing tearout or smoothing tricky grain. For finer cuts, I pull the scraper to flatten any dished areas and leave a surface ready for finishing.

To push the scraper, hold it with your fingers on the short edges and your thumbs together in the middle of the back, about ½ in. or so above the cutting edge. Use your thumbs to create a slight bow along the bottom edge. The deeper the bow, the more aggressive the cut. Conventional wisdom says to start by holding the scraper vertically and angling it forward until you feel the burr bite into the wood. It works, but in my experience, it's easier for beginners to start with the scraper held at about 60° and, while pushing, slowly increase the angle until the burr begins to cut the wood. Then push forward in one smooth motion to get continuous, paper-thin shavings.

To pull the scraper, place your fingers on the far side and your thumbs on the face closest to you. Unlike when pushing, your thumbs should be positioned higher on the face of the scraper and your fingers lower. A pulled scraper is held with the edge bowed only enough to prevent the corners from digging into the wood. Some woodworkers avoid this problem by rounding the corners with a file or grinder.

A scraped surface that's finish ready

In my shop, a card scraper touches virtually every surface of a project and is almost always the last tool to do so before the finish goes on. If I'm working easily planed, straight-grained stock, I typically clean up jointer and planer marks on larger surfaces with a handplane, then use the scraper to remove plane tracks and clean up tearout. To ensure

Pulling leaves a flatter surface. Align your fingertips behind the cutting edge to apply uniform pressure.

Use caution near edges. Avoid letting the scraper dig into the workpiece edges and leave them ragged. Here, Teague bows the scraper enough to concentrate cutting pressure in the center of the workpiece.

a uniform appearance under a finish, I give all the surfaces at least a light scraping. In general, I scrape the entire surface using a push stroke, then flatten the slightly dished area using a pull stroke.

For stock with trickier grain, such as bird's-eye or burl, I skip handplaning altogether. A scraper is much easier to control than a handplane, and there is almost no chance of tearout.

In any case, if the milling marks are especially heavy, I usually start by power sanding to 120 grit. I prefer the way a scraped surface looks under a finish, so at this point I thoroughly brush or vacuum away the sanding dust and scrape until the entire surface is uniform.

Restore the edge

A dull scraper takes more effort to push and a steeper cutting angle. It also creates dust instead of wide shavings.

Fortunately, it's possible to restore the burr several times simply by reburnishing the face and then the edge in the same way you initially turned the burr. After four to six burnishings, the metal becomes brittle and you need a new surface. Return the scraper to the vise and start over with a file, removing any nicks along the edge that you've created by scraping. Then burnish the faces and edges to draw and turn new burrs.

Because each tune-up removes so little steel, I still use the first scraper I bought a dozen years ago. Sandpaper, however, usually wears out in minutes.

You Need a Cabinet Scraper

PHILIP C. LOWE

Unlike the more familiar card scraper, the cabinet scraper is not made to leave a finished surface. Instead, it's a rougher tool, used to remove tearout and machining marks created by the jointer and planer and tracks left by handplanes before you begin final surface preparations with sandpaper and a card scraper.

It's a bit of a quirky tool. Although the blade looks like a card scraper and cuts with a hook, it's a bit thicker and mounted in a body similar to that of a spokeshave. But the sole is larger than a spokeshave's. This bigger sole prevents you from creating a divot—which can happen with a card scraper if you concentrate too much on any one spot—because it forces you to work a larger area of the surface.

A cabinet scraper does a great job if set up properly. I'll show you how to sharpen the blade and how to set it to take nice shavings. I'll also give you a few tips for using it and for correcting some common problems.

Hook the blade

Although the cabinet scraper's blade is beveled (45°), it actually cuts with a hook turned onto the cutting edge.

File the Edge

Use a 10-in. mill bastard file to expose fresh steel. Clamping the blade in a hand screw clamped in your bench vise (left) raises it to a good working height. Check that the edge remains straight as you file it.

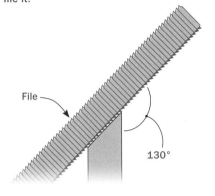

File

130°

File and hone the bevel. A good hook starts with fresh steel and a polished bevel. Repeat this process every time you turn the hook, as using the scraper hardens the edge too much to allow you to re-turn it.

Hone the bevel freehand. The blade is too big for a guide. To maintain the bevel angle, lock your elbows against your body and rock your legs forward and back.

Don't forget the back. Polish it to the same level that you polish the bevel. Lowe works the bevel and back before moving to the next stone.

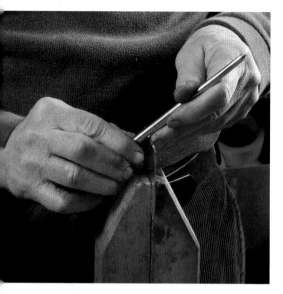

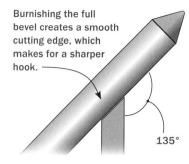

Burnishing the full bevel creates a smooth cutting edge, which makes for a sharper hook.

135°

Roll the hook. Get a strong hook by forming it slowly, rolling it a bit more with each stroke. To start, burnish the entire bevel. Take several strokes back and forth across the bevel to flatten any scratches that might remain after honing.

Raising the angle of the burnisher with each pass actually rolls the hook, rather than simply pushing it down. That makes the hook stronger.

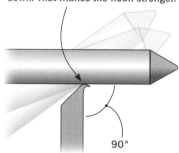

90°

Work the hook. Take several strokes, raising the burnisher 5° to 10° with each stroke, taking the final stroke with the burnisher 90° to the blade.

Correcting the angle of the entire burr creates a better cutting edge.

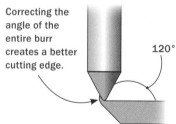

120°

Now fine-tune the hook's angle. It's fairly easy to roll the hook too far or to roll it at an inconsistent angle. To fix this, you need a burnisher with a pointed tip. Run the tip along the hook, which brings it to a consistent 120° angle, perfect for scraping.

After filing the bevel to expose fresh steel, hone the bevel and polish the back on your sharpening stones. I work my way through four grits—1,000, 5,000, 8,000, and 16,000—but you could use similar grits and just go through 8,000.

Now you can turn the hook. Hold the burnisher at 45° and burnish the bevel to remove and flatten out any remaining scratches. Next, take several strokes along the cutting edge, raising the burnisher with each stroke until it is square to the blade.

After turning the hook, I lay the blade flat on my bench with the hook facing up and run the tip of my burnisher along the hook. The tip is shaped like a cone, and adjusts the hook to a consistent angle, improving its cutting ability (You can buy a burnisher like this from me at www. furnituremakingclasses.com).

The blade is ready to cut shavings now, so put it back in. Tighten the clamping bar and set the cut depth with the thumbscrew.

Scrape before cutting parts to size

As you scrape, apply even downward pressure with both hands and be sure not to scrape more from one area than others. Also, hold the tool at a slight angle to prevent the blade from grabbing and catching, especially near the corners. I push the scraper, but it can be pulled.

Work from the ends in toward the center, because if you scrape down the length of the part, there is a good chance the blade will catch at the far end, leaving a crease that is difficult to remove. You'll end up scraping against the grain on part of the board, which will lift the grain and leave a rougher surface than scraping with the grain. But that's OK. The cabinet scraper isn't meant to produce a finished surface and you'll be smoothing afterward.

Set up for fluffy shavings. Insert the blade into the scraper body from beneath, with the hook facing toward the clamping bar. Clamp the blade in place. With the scraper on your bench, press down on the blade so it's bottoming out on the bench. Tighten both screws evenly.

2. Tighten the blade at front.

3. Thumbscrew at back adjusts depth of cut.

1. Insert the blade from the bottom.

Set the depth of cut. Turning the thumbscrew clockwise flexes the blade and increases the depth of cut. However, the greater the blade's flex, the narrower the cut, so go easy and take wide, fluffy shavings unless the tearout or machine marks are deep.

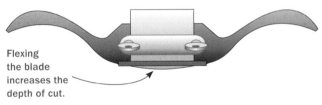

Flexing the blade increases the depth of cut.

However, because the plane's sole doesn't get a lot of support at the start of the cut, you might not get a great surface there. To avoid this problem, scrape parts before you cut them to their final dimensions. You can cut away any bad surfaces around the ends afterward.

Blade chatter can be caused by uneven pressure from the clamping bar or roughness on the surface of the bar that clamps against the blade. Use a mill file to smooth it, and adjust the thumbscrews to even out the pressure.

Works great on difficult woods. Because of its cutting angle, the cabinet scraper cleans up figured woods, eliminating the tearout left by machines and handplanes.

4 Planes for Joinery

VIC TESOLIN

At just 170 sq. ft., my shop is—without question—small. When I first moved into it, I was forced to think carefully about which machines were essential and which I could do without. In the end, only my bandsaw, drill press, and thickness planer survived the cut. As a result, most of my woodworking, including all of the joinery, is done with hand tools.

After I made that decision, it didn't take long to realize that to cut joinery by hand I'd need more than just my backsaw and a set of chisels. So over time I added some specialty planes to my collection. With these planes—shoulder, router, rabbet, and plow—I'm able to knock out just about any traditional furniture joint quickly and accurately. Here I'll demonstrate how I use each of these planes in my furniture making, and I'll give you some tips on setting them up for best results.

Shoulder plane: Fine-tunes tenons

Cutting the mortise-and-tenon joint by hand means sawing the shoulders and the cheeks with a backsaw. And unless your saw work is perfect, you'll need to trim both the cheeks and the shoulders to get the tenon to fit the mortise tightly with no gaps. This is where the shoulder plane comes in. As its name suggests, it excels at trimming shoulders. Set for a light cut, it can also do a good job of trimming the cheeks. Your first shoulder

Align the blade to the body. To avoid creating a stepped corner, the iron must be flush with the side of the plane that's in the corner. A blade that's a bit wider than the body is easy to set up. With the cap iron loose and the plane on its side, press the blade down against the bench, then retighten the cap iron.

plane should have a ¾-in.-wide blade. It's small enough for shoulders, but wide enough to trim most cheeks in two passes. Comfort is important, too, so give the plane a spin before buying it if you can. Whether you buy new or used, check that the blade is slightly wider than the body, and that the sole is square to both sides. Finally, look for an adjustable mouth, so you can tighten it for light shavings.

Shoulder Plane

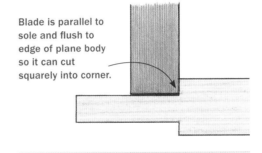

Blade is parallel to sole and flush to edge of plane body so it can cut squarely into corner.

Stand up for cheeks. You have to flatten the cheeks before trimming the shoulders. To prevent the cheeks from tapering, overlap cuts and work carefully to your layout lines.

Lay down for shoulders. With the rail laid horizontally, the tenon's cheek becomes a broad support surface for the plane, making it much easier to trim the shoulder than if you held the rail vertical and tried to balance the plane on the narrow shoulder.

Router plane: Guarantees flat-bottomed cuts

Though designed for a very specific task—to trim the bottom of a recess flat and parallel to the surface of the workpiece—the router plane is quite versatile. It can be used to clean up the bottoms of dadoes and to cut mortises for hinges and inlay. It also can be used to trim tenon cheeks. Working from both sides of the rail, you end up with a tenon that's perfectly centered and cheeks that are parallel to one another. Two features I recommend are a depth stop, which makes it easier to set the blade's cutting depth, and a fence, which allows you to work parallel to edges. Look for a fence that allows you to work both straight and concave edges. As for size, large router planes are good for most furniture-size joinery and larger hinge mortises. Small ones are great for inlay and smaller hinge mortises.

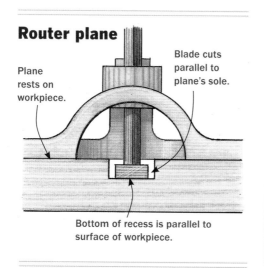

Router plane

Plane rests on workpiece.

Blade cuts parallel to plane's sole.

Bottom of recess is parallel to surface of workpiece.

Hinge mortises. Start by marking the mortise depth. Use a wheel or cutting gauge set to the hinge leaf's thickness.

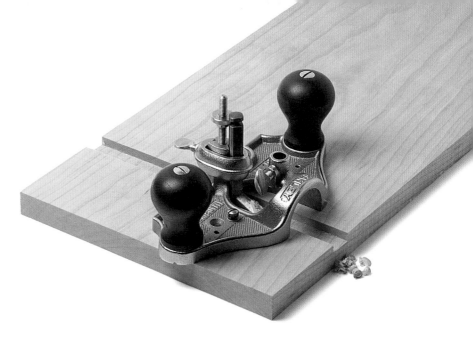

Set the blade depth. Put the blade's cutting edge into the knifed line, then lock it in.

Chisel the waste. After lightly chopping across the grain down the length of the mortise, clear out the waste by chiseling in from the open side. Don't attempt to pare down to the mortise's full depth.

Plane to final depth. Balance the plane on the door's edge, wrapping your fingers around the stile, then come straight in. The blade is set to the final depth, so one series of overlapping cuts does the job.

Tenons. You're only roughing out the tenon at this point, so there's no need to saw to the line (far left). After setting the blade's depth of cut just like you did for the hinge mortise, clean up the cut with the router plane (left). Press the plane firmly onto the rail, and then pivot the plane with the outboard hand, bringing the blade over the tenon in an arc.

Stopped dadoes. A chisel removes the waste in two steps. After defining the dado's sides with a knife followed by a chisel, work from the center out and down to chip out the waste quickly (top left). Use a chisel, bevel down, to get rid of the triangular ridge of waste that remains after the first step (above). Two to three passes should be enough. Stop when there's just a bit left, and trim down to the final depth with the router plane (bottom left).

Rabbet plane: Ideal for case joinery

Rabbets show up in furniture making more than you might think. Case and cabinet backs typically fit into rabbets, drawer bottoms are rabbeted to fit into their grooves, and panels— whether for a door or casework—are often rabbeted to fit into the frame's grooves. To cut a rabbet, you need a plane with a blade that extends just past the edge of the body (so that it cuts cleanly into the corner), a fence to control the rabbet's width, a depth stop to

Rabbet Plane

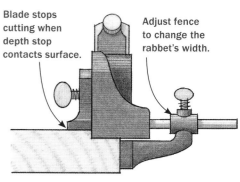

Blade stops cutting when depth stop contacts surface.

Adjust fence to change the rabbet's width.

Start at the far end. As you work back toward the near end, both the fence and the blade will guide the plane. The added tracking from the blade is key while the rabbet is still shallow.

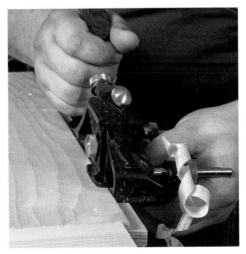

Concentrate on the fence. To cut a vertical wall, keep firm, sideways pressure on the plane's fence. Push gently on the tote with the other hand to move the plane through the cut.

Simple setup. To prevent tearout when cutting cross-grain rabbets use the nicker, making sure it's aligned with the blade's edge (top). It severs the fibers cleanly ahead of the blade. A stop on the side controls the rabbet's depth. It's easiest to set it with a rule (center). But set the fence, which determines the rabbet's width, directly from the workpiece (above).

determine its depth, and a nicker in front of the blade to sever wood fibers when cutting a cross-grain rabbet. This is exactly what you get with a rabbet plane. It's also nice, but not necessary, to have a skewed blade, which makes it easier to work across the grain.

Plow plane: Cuts flawless grooves

Need to make a drawer or a frame-and-panel door? You'll have to cut some grooves. To cut grooves accurately and repeatedly, get a plow plane. Like a rabbet plane, the plow has a fence and depth stop, allowing you to locate the groove precisely and control its depth. You can also get blades of different widths, so you can cut different size grooves.

Plow Plane

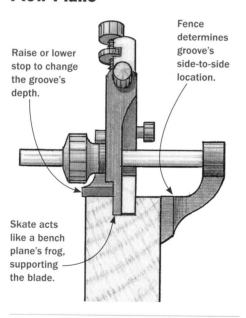

Raise or lower stop to change the groove's depth.

Fence determines groove's side-to-side location.

Skate acts like a bench plane's frog, supporting the blade.

Fence locates the cutter. Tesolin scribes a centerline for the groove, centers the cutter on the line, and then pushes the fence against the workpiece, tightening the locknuts with his other hand.

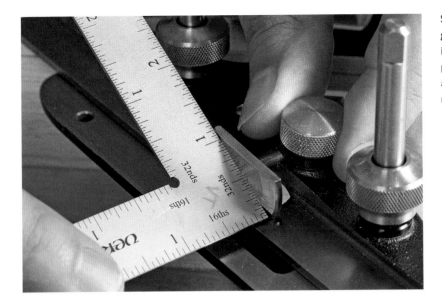

Stop determines the groove's depth. Because it's easier and more precise, set the stop with a rule rather than with a mark on the workpiece.

Apply pressure to the fence. To get clean vertical walls, keep your fingers low and press the fence against the workpiece. It takes very little force to push the plane forward, so go light on the tote.

Get to Know Japanese Handplanes

ANDREW HUNTER

I first took the plunge into the unfamiliar waters of the kanna, or Japanese handplane, more than 15 years ago. Learning to use one took time and dedication, but the reward of the shimmering surface it leaves was well worth it. There is more to Japanese handplanes than can be expressed in a single chapter, but my aim here is to provide a kind of diving board for anyone else interested in taking the plunge. I promise the water is delightful.

What makes these planes different

Japanese planes cut on the pull stroke, and it can take a while to adapt to this, though when you do you'll discover it gives you both more power and more control. But the first challenge with a Japanese plane is that it isn't ready to use out of the box. You get great ingredients, but it is up to you to make the tool perform well. This responsibility might seem daunting at first, but as you grow more comfortable with your plane you will be glad for the control.

The heart and soul of the Japanese plane is its massive tapered blade. A descendant of the samurai sword, the blade has a thin layer of superhard steel laminated to a thick layer of softer mild steel or iron. The hard steel provides a cutting edge of unparalleled sharpness, while the softer backing metal dampens the heat and vibration of the cut. The flat face of the blade—the hard steel side—comes hollowed at the center. So when you lay it on a stone for flattening, only a

Tapping Out the Blade

Through repeated sharpening of the bevel, the front flat on the back of a Japanese blade will begin to disappear. The solution is to tap the layer of soft steel above the cutting edge to press the hard steel downward slightly, which presents more hard steel at the edge for flattening. This particular blade has been ground flat too often without tapping out and now has wide side flats that slow the flattening process.

Tap, then flatten the back. When tapping the blade, be careful not to crack the hard steel. Strike the upper half of the bevel with light blows, backing them up from below with a block or anvil.

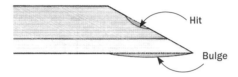

Hit

Bulge

---

small amount of metal at the edges contacts the stone, greatly speeding the process.

The blade fits snugly into angled grooves on either side of the body, or block, of the plane. On a typical Japanese plane, the blade, which is inserted bevel down, is bedded at around 39°. All of my blades are in this range except a 45° finish plane I use on difficult grain. You can order blocks with specific bedding angles or make your own.

The blade is adjusted with light hammer blows. To advance the blade, strike its blunt back edge, favoring the left or right to effect skew adjustment. To withdraw the blade, strike the plane block on its chamfered back edge, alternating taps left and right.

The chipbreaker is wedged in place beneath a removable pin. Like the blade, the chipbreaker is adjusted with a hammer. Its purpose is twofold. It exerts pressure on the blade, stabilizing it and helping reduce chatter. But also its steep secondary bevel contacts the shaving right after it is cut,

Prepare the blade. Start by cleaning up the bevel. The thick Japanese blade makes for a wide bevel and easier freehand sharpening. Honing guides made for Japanese blades are another option. The sharpening goes quickly, as most of the bevel is soft metal.

bending it back and greatly reducing the chance of tearout.

Setup starts with the blade

There are five steps in setting up a new Japanese plane: shaping the blade, fitting the

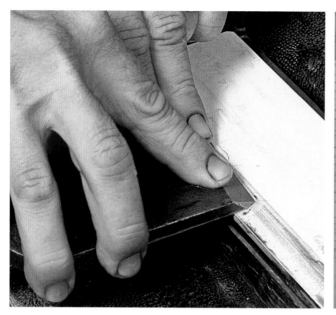

Flatten the back. The hard steel back of a new blade comes hollowed, leaving only narrow areas around the perimeter to be polished during flattening. The narrower you keep these flats, the more efficient your sharpening will be.

blade into the block, fitting the chipbreaker, tuning the sole, and adjusting the mouth opening.

Begin shaping the blade by addressing the bevel. Most blades come with a bevel of about 28°, a good standard angle. If you're happy with that, you can move on to the back; if you want to change it, do so now. Next, flatten the back of the blade. Rub it on a flat, medium-grit stone and then read the scratch pattern. You are looking for consistent scratches across the entire front edge. If there is a spot with no scratches it may be tempting to grind the whole surface on a coarse stone. But each time you do, you'll widen the side flats and shrink the hollow, increasing the amount of hard steel you have to flatten with each sharpening. Instead, Japanese blades are usually "tapped out"—struck on the bevel with light hammer blows so the blade bulges slightly on the back, presenting a little more hard steel for flattening.

With each sharpening of the bevel, the front flat on the back gets slightly narrower. Over time, it will disappear altogether; when

it does, instead of grinding the whole back you can tap out the blade again and grind briefly to reestablish the front flat. In this way, the narrow flats can be maintained for the life of the blade.

When this preliminary shaping is done, the blade is ready to be fitted to the block. Final sharpening will happen in the end.

Fit the blade into the block

A new plane blade will not perfectly fit its block. It is up to you to get the fit just right. As you insert the blade, flat side up and bevel down, it is captured in two shallow, angled grooves. The upper shoulder of these grooves, against which the flattened face of the blade presses, is the bedding angle for the blade and should not be adjusted. Instead, you'll shape the broad ramp the blade rests on. The better the fit of blade to ramp, the less the blade will vibrate.

To begin, remove the pin and cover the front face of the blade with a graphite slurry. Tap the blade into the block until it's snug. Then remove the blade and study the black

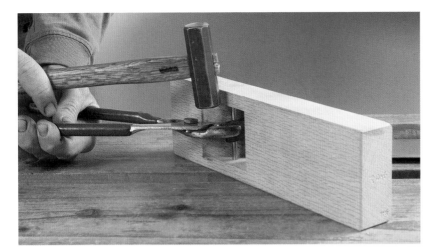

Seat the blade in the block. To start remove the pin. With the plane over a dog hole, grip the retaining pin with padded pliers and tap to remove it.

Look for high spots. Cover the face and the side edges of the blade with a graphite and light oil slurry (left). Tap the blade into the block and remove (right). Black marks reveal high spots.

Pare high spots and repeat. Lightly scrape and pare away black marks on the ramp (above) and at the sides (right). Continue this process until the blade fits just shy of protruding.

The goal is dark and even. The ramp should be covered with graphite. It's most important to have black along the edges and front.

Preparing the chipbreaker. After flattening the back (left) and working a primary bevel, Hunter creates a steep secondary bevel (below). To do so, he holds the chipbreaker still and moves the stone, guided by a bevel gauge.

marks left on the ramp where the fit was tight. Lightly pare these spots and reinsert the blade, repeating the process until the blade is just shy of protruding. I like the fit to be tight; it will ease up with time. If the fit becomes too loose either from age or overzealous tuning, glue a paper or veneer shim to the ramp.

Shape and fit the chipbreaker

Now it's time to work on the chipbreaker. First, sharpen it like a blade, with a flat back and a straight bevel. Then create a narrow secondary bevel of around 60°. This steep surface is what bends the chip back. The chipbreaker has two ears at the top end that bend downward to contact the blade; don't flatten these.

Next, with the blade out of the block, rest the chipbreaker in position on it and check for wobble. If there is any, you'll adjust the ears, either hammering one ear down to make it protrude farther or filing the other back to make it protrude less. The choice depends on the fit of the blade and chipbreaker in the block. So tap the blade

Breaking point. The chipbreaker's secondary bevel, which can be as narrow as 1/32 in., bends the wood fibers back just after they've been cut for a very clean shave.

Eliminate wobble. Rest the chipbreaker in place on the blade. There should be no gaps across the front edge, and the back corners, or ears, should sit on the blade without rocking. Make adjustments by bending an ear down with a hammer or filing it back.

into the block just shy of protruding, then press the chipbreaker under the pin with your fingers. A few light taps with a hammer should bring it to the front edge of the blade. Adjust the ears until the fit is snug. Then remove the blade and chipbreaker from the block to be sure they fit together without wobbling.

Create landings on the sole

For best performance, any bench plane needs to have a bearing surface that is true and applies pressure to the wood fibers just before they are cut. With Japanese planes this is cleverly accomplished by relieving the sole so that only a few gliding strips, or landings, contact the workpiece. Not only do

Get your landings in the same plane. Start by flattening the whole sole. Then, once you've hollowed it, leaving only narrow landings to contact the workpiece, use winding sticks to be certain the landings are in the same plane.

Sole landings

Relieve the sole so only narrow strips, or landings, contact the workpiece.

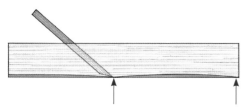

Smoothing planes have two landings, one at the leading edge and one just ahead of the blade. This ensures maximum pressure right ahead of the cut.

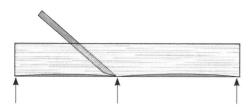

For a jointer plane, used to make a board perfectly flat, an additional landing at the trailing end of the body is necessary.

The hollows shouldn't be deep. Check the sole with a straightedge. You should see only a hair of light. Tune the sole with the blade and breaker in place, but retracted slightly.

these narrow landings magnify the pressure applied by the user and deliver it just where it's needed, but they also are easily adjusted true to one another.

To work on the sole, keep the blade and breaker in place, since the pressure they exert slightly distorts the block. Start by making the whole sole true so that the landings start out in plane with one another. This can be done using winding sticks and planes or with sandpaper and a dead-flat surface.

The hollowing is best done with scrapers. Once that's done, check to be sure the landing ahead of the blade is flat. Then use winding sticks to see if the other landings are in plane with it and adjust accordingly. Finally, use a straightedge along the length of the block to be sure the hollows are sufficiently relieved. Periodically the condition of the sole should be checked.

Adjust the mouth and throat

You want the mouth open just enough to admit shavings, but not so much that the benefits of exerting pressure ahead of the cut are lost. Adjust the opening with a chisel. Also, be sure the blade's cutting edge is not wider than the throat, or shavings will jam. Reduce the width by grinding back the two bevels at the front corners of the blade. These adjustments will need to be periodically maintained.

Give the blade a final sharpening and have at it. On flat stock, your plane should pull a thin, consistent shaving with only moderate effort. The plane should be very sensitive now and the blade needs to protrude only a hair. If the blade is protruding but you are not getting a cut, recheck the landings and hollows.

Create the sole profile. With a Japanese scraper plane Hunter creates long, shallow reliefs, leaving ½-in.-wide landings across the sole. A card scraper also works fine.

Focused attention. The area behind the mouth can bulge due to pressure from the blade and breaker. Relieve it with a chisel.

Address each side of the mouth. Shallow relief cuts eliminate having to work this area when shaping the sole.

Adjust the blade width and mouth

Grind the blade so the cutting edge is the width of the throat.

Throat

Mouth

Limit the width of the blade's cutting edge. It should not be more than the width of the throat, or shavings will jam. Reduce its width by grinding back the bevels at the front corners of the blade.

Adjust the opening. The gap between blade and body should be just wide enough to allow shavings through. Use a chisel and guide block to adjust it.

Using a Japanese Plane: The Potent Pull Stroke

Using a Japanese plane is similar to using a Japanese saw in that they both cut with a pull stroke. The plane gives you greater control as it is drawn in. Your hands should be strong but relaxed. Keep the energy out of your shoulders and elbows and draw back with your legs and abdomen. You are not aiming for an explosive power but a controlled, steady strength.

For short strokes, keep the plane close to your center where you have the most control. For longer cuts, reach out to the end of your balance and draw back in to your center. Your body should be like a spring that is straightened and then recoils, using the power from the large muscles of your back and core. Sink into your legs; they provide the stability to counter the pulling force. Without lifting the plane, reposition your feet and repeat. With practice you will be able to walk backward while keeping the connection to the cut with your center. There is a lot to take in when first learning to use a kanna. Hang in there; it will become second nature and your boards will be shining in no time.

Short strokes or long. On shorter boards, keep the plane close to your center, where you have the most control. For long cuts, reach out to the end of your balance and draw back in to your center.

Get a grip. Hold the plane with your dominant hand about halfway between the blade and the leading edge, favoring the blade. Most of the pressure is applied with this hand and care must be given to distribute it equally across the block. The other hand supports the blade and helps with the pulling.

SETTING THE BLADE

Advance the blade by tapping on its blunt back edge. Withdraw it by tapping the chamfered back upper corner of the plane block. Adjust for skew with taps to the blade's back corners.

Turn Your Shoulder Plane into a Star Performer

PHILIP C. LOWE

In my shop, the shoulder plane is the go-to tool for trimming tenon cheeks. The low-angle, bevel-up blade works great across the grain. And because the blade is as wide as the plane body, it can cut all the way into the corner where the cheek meets the shoulder. This ability is also essential when I use my plane on rabbets.

However, despite its name, I typically don't use a shoulder plane on tenon shoulders. That's because most tenon shoulders are shorter than the plane is long—not to mention narrow. It's hard to balance the plane on the shoulder and get a good cut. Instead, I use a chisel. To see how I do it, take a look at "4 Chisel Tricks" (p. 116).

For best results on tenon cheeks, a shoulder plane needs a flat sole and sides that are square to it. Also, the width of the blade should match the width of the body. You might think they come that way from the manufacturer, but it's actually common for

the blade to be a bit wider. So, I'll show you how adjust the blade's width and give you some tips for setting it up for square cuts.

If you don't already own a shoulder plane, get one that's at least 1 in. wide. Most tenons are between 1 in. and 1½ in. long, and a narrower plane is more likely to taper the tenon.

Check the plane body, then tweak the blade

A shoulder plane won't cut a square corner unless it has a dead-flat sole and sides that are exactly 90° to it. So, the first time you pick up the plane, check the sole with a straightedge and use a combination square to check that the sides are square to the sole. If the sole

Three step tune-up. Intended to cut into square corners, a shoulder plane needs a flat sole, square sides, and a blade as wide as the plane. To start, check that the body is straight and square. Hold the plane up toward a light source. Light sneaking between the plane and a rule means it's not flat. Replace the rule with a combination square to determine if the sides are 90° to the sole.

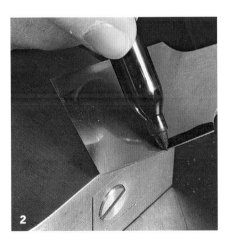

Tweak the blade's width. Ink along one edge. It's much easier to see the scribe line you'll create against a dark background than against the steel of the blade.

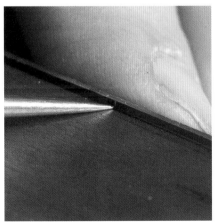

Mark the sole's width. Lowe uses the scribe from his combination square, holding its tip slightly above the plane body as a precaution against grinding the blade too narrow.

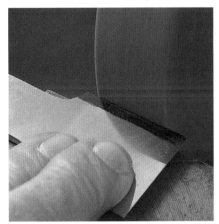

Grind to the line. Set the tool rest at 90° to the wheel. Grind away most of the excess, then smooth the rough edge on your sharpening stones.

(Continued on p. 60)

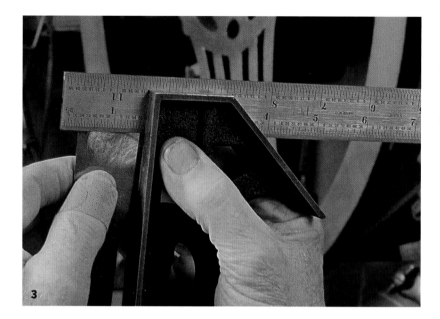

Square the cutting edge. Look into the light and register the square on the factory edge of the blade (the one you didn't grind). If the cutting edge is out of square, regrind it.

isn't flat or the sides aren't square to it, return the plane. Correcting those problems is not worth the hassle.

After checking the body of the plane, turn your focus to the blade. Take it out of the plane, then lay the plane on its side on a flat surface. Hold the flat side of the blade against the plane's sole and look to make sure the blade is wider than the body. If it's not, send the plane back. If the blade is too narrow, one side won't cut into the corner, creating a wider step and pushing the plane farther away from the shoulder with each pass.

However, a blade that's too wide is also a problem, because it can dig into the shoulder. Ideally, the blade should be the same width as the body, but if it's 0.001 in. to 0.002 in. wider, that's OK.

Mark one edge of the flat side of the blade with a permanent marker. Then, with the

Set up for a square cut. A shoulder plane's primary use is to trim joinery, so it's critical that it takes a shaving the full width of the blade and of a consistent depth. To set the blade in the body, pinch the blade between your fingers to center it, and tighten the hold-down to keep it in place (left). Then adjust the mouth, if that's possible on your plane (above).

plane on its side and the blade pressed against the sole, scribe the body's width on the blade.

Grind it down with a bench grinder (or on your sharpening stones). It's critical that the two sides of the blade are parallel to one another, so use calipers to check them as you grind. Next, check whether the cutting edge is square to the factory edge. If not, grind it square. Finally, sharpen the blade. I recommend a hollow grind for the bevel. Because of the blade's shape, it doesn't fit well in honing guides. The two high points created by the hollow grind make it easier to hone the blade freehand.

Set up for a square shaving

Now that the blade is sharp, put it back in the plane. When sliding it into the throat, take care not to nick the edge and be certain that the adjuster mates solidly with the blade. Visually check that it's centered in the throat.

Next, square the cutting edge in the mouth. First, get it roughly set by turning the plane sole up with the blade projecting beyond the sole. Sight down the sole of

Narrow shavings are bad. A blade that's cutting square takes a shaving across its width. This blade is cutting too deep on the right.

the plane from the front. Make lateral adjustments to the blade until it projects equally across its entire width.

Now retract the blade so that it doesn't cut. Then begin pushing the plane across a piece of scrap and increase the depth of cut

Here's how to fix the problem. Loosen the hold-down just enough to allow you to shift the blade's tang. Move it toward the side of the blade that wasn't cutting (left). When the blade is cutting square, it cuts a full-width shaving that has a uniform thickness (above).

Keep the plane vertical in use. A simple bench hook holds workpieces on their side so you can hold the plane upright, where it is easier to control. For straight tenon cheeks, first place the toe of the plane on the tenon and slide it forward until the blade just touches. Then take a shaving, keeping even pressure on the plane throughout the cut.

as you go. When you start to get a shaving, notice where the blade is cutting. If it's making a square cut, the shaving will be the full width of the blade. If not, adjust the tang of the blade in the direction of the corner that isn't cutting. Pinch your fingers around the plane and blade near the cutting edge to keep that end still. Loosen the hold-down and nudge the tang over. Tighten the hold-down. Test and adjust the blade until it's right. Finally, set the mouth—if that's possible on your plane—narrow for figured and hard woods and wider for soft woods.

Start at the shoulder. And don't overlap cuts. Otherwise, you'll get cheeks that aren't parallel.

For rabbets, rotate the board (not the plane). For the wall parallel to the board's face (left), clamp the board between benchdogs and use your off hand to keep the plane tight against the rabbet's vertical wall. Use a vise for the other wall (above). With the board on edge, there's no need to lay the plane on its side.

Got a Skew Chisel?

GARRETT HACK

About 30 years ago at a tool sale, I bought a fine Marples® bevel-edged chisel with about a third of the blade snapped off. I took it home and ground a new edge at an 18° skew. I still have that chisel, and I can't imagine cutting dovetails by hand without it.

Nothing better for reaching into tight spots.
The angled tip is ideal for precise cuts deep into tight corners (the skew angle actually forces it into the corner), and for long paring cuts. The chisel is adept at cleaning out waste between double tenons as well as for cleaning up the corners at the base of a tenon (left).

Dovetail corners. The tip of the skew easily shears away the end grain in a half-blind dovetail (left), and pares the long-grain areas, too (above).

You can buy bevel-edge skew chisels—they're often sold in pairs for between $60 and $130—but it's far less expensive to make your own. All it takes is a flea-market chisel (⅜ in. or ½ in. works well) or an extra chisel you already own. And there's no reason to make a pair. A single skew works great. I use mine bevel down and bevel up to get into left and right corners.

Making a skew chisel involves blunting the tip at the skew angle, grinding the bevel, and then honing. It's not difficult at all.

Subtle Angle Is Better

A skew of 18° may seem shallow, but a more acute skew will tend to push the chisel sideways. It will be harder to control and undercutting a pin or the sidewall of a mortise might become an issue.

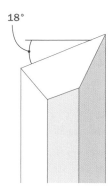

18°

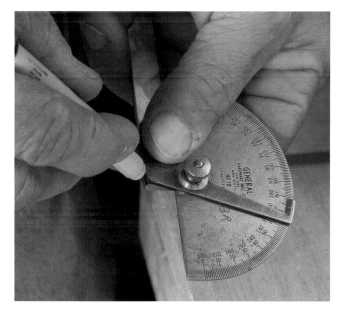

Turn an old chisel into a specialized tool. Hack sharpens his skew chisel to an angle of 18°. It's no more difficult than grinding a new edge on a badly nicked chisel. Use a fine-point felt-tipped marker to draw the skew angle on the back of the chisel.

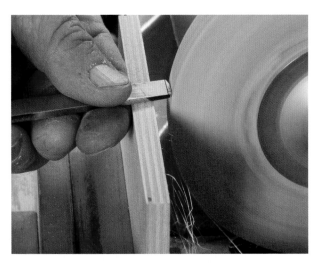

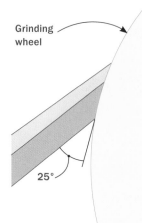

Grinding wheel

25°

Blunt the tip. The safest way to make this heavy grind is to hold the chisel horizontal to the grinder and create a blunt edge at the new skew angle. Go slowly and never heat the edge hotter than you can touch or you risk ruining the temper.

Grind the bevel. Set the tool rest to 25° and carefully grind the bevel using the blunt edge as a guide. Grind lightly and intermittently, as heat will build quickly at the fine leading edge.

Relive the Sides

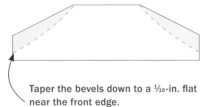

Taper the bevels down to a 1/16-in. flat near the front edge.

Freehand works best. Hone the bevel through progressive grits. Also smooth the relieved areas on the long edges of the blade.

Thin the edges to improve the reach. Grinding the steep sides along the blade creates a narrow edge that lets the chisel reach into the tight corners at the bottom of a dovetail.

Choosing and Using Japanese Chisels

JOHN REED FOX

The machine area of my shop is stocked with Western woodworking machines. But over at my workbench, all the hand tools are Japanese. Just as it's hard to beat hefty Western machines, I think Japanese hand tools clearly outperform their Western counterparts. When it comes to chisels, the Japanese variety takes a sharper, more durable edge than Western chisels; these tools simply work better and for a longer period of time.

What makes them so good?

Japanese chisels, like other Japanese edge tools, are laminated, and this is the key. A thin layer of very hard and finely tuned high-carbon steel—the cutting edge—is forge-welded to a thicker piece of iron or low-carbon steel that forms the body of the blade. The thick layer of softer metal provides mass and shock dampening and prevents the hard, brittle steel from fracturing.

When you buy a new Japanese chisel, there's some setup to do before you can put it to work—flattening the back, creating the cutting bevel, and setting the hoop (for an explanation of that process, see p. 74). Here I'll explain the anatomy of Japanese bench chisels, walk you through the various types, and give you guidelines and specific suggestions for which chisels to buy. Good-quality Japanese chisels are still made one

Basic Features

Nearly all Japanese-style chisels share a common anatomy, give or take the hoop, which is not found on dedicated paring chisels. But there are interesting variations in the blades, some significant and some not.

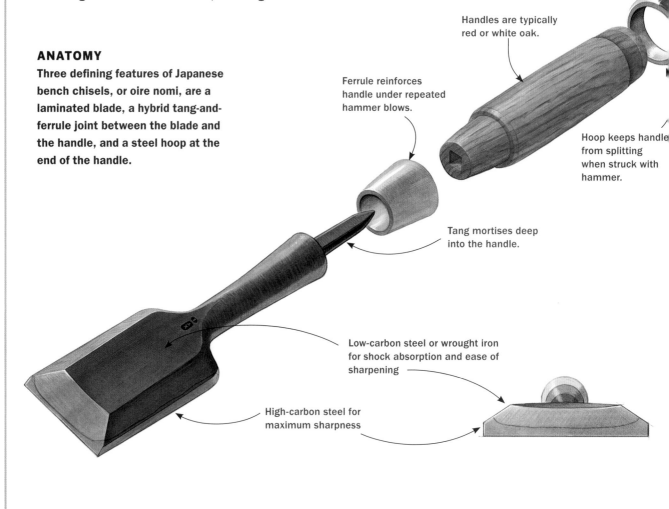

ANATOMY
Three defining features of Japanese bench chisels, or oire nomi, are a laminated blade, a hybrid tang-and-ferrule joint between the blade and the handle, and a steel hoop at the end of the handle.

Handles are typically red or white oak.

Ferrule reinforces handle under repeated hammer blows.

Hoop keeps handle from splitting when struck with hammer.

Tang mortises deep into the handle.

Low-carbon steel or wrought iron for shock absorption and ease of sharpening

High-carbon steel for maximum sharpness

at a time by individual blacksmiths in small shops, and I like the idea that while buying the best tool I can find I'm also helping keep an age-old craft alive.

Using a Japanese chisel
Using Japanese chisels doesn't present anything like the radical shift users experience when going from Western to Japanese planes and saws. Japanese bench chisels are generally shorter than Western chisels and have a different feel and balance, but you'll work with them in the same ways.

One slight difference in use is due to the hollows on the back of the blade. When you are paring with a Japanese chisel and

PROFILES

The Japanese bench chisel comes in a variety of blade profiles. These are four of the most common and useful.

KAKU UCHI

An old style with only slightly raked sides, this profile delivers maximum power for chopping but is less versatile when paring.

MENTORI

The most common blade profile, it combines heft for chopping and striking with side bevels for paring access.

KINARI

With longer bevels than the mentori, this more delicate profile is excellent for paring dovetails but still retains enough mass for effective chopping.

SHINOGI

The low, wide-beveled blade profile affords excellent access when paring in tight spaces. It is used only on push chisels—unhooped chisels not meant for striking.

BACKS

You'll find one or more hollows on the back of a Japanese chisel. They make flattening and honing the hard, high-carbon steel back easier.

FINISHES

Depending on the maker, the body of a Japanese chisel may be finished in a variety of ways. The finishes are decorative and don't affect functionality. From left: polished, or file-finish; black; mokume, or wood-grained; and hammered.

the back is registered against a flat surface, you have to adapt to the fact that you don't have the full width to ride on as you would with a Western chisel. Also note that Japanese chisels should never be used with a prying motion, as this action risks breaking the edge.

Sharpening the laminated blade may actually be easier than what you're used to. Because the thin steel cutting edge needs to be fully supported, the bevel of a Japanese chisel shouldn't be hollow-ground or given a microbevel—the whole bevel stays flat and the whole thing is honed at each sharpening. But since the backing iron is soft, sharpening

Using Japanese chisels. With their super-sharp blades and hooped handles, Japanese chisels perform both chopping and paring tasks with ease and accuracy. Its hooped handle lets the Japanese chisel take a pounding. A steel striking hammer, or dai dogyu, delivers a sharp, accurate blow.

Precision paring. Japanese bench chisels are superb for paring but shouldn't be used with a prying action, which could chip the very hard cutting edge.

Specialty tools in action. The shinogi push chisel (above) excels at paring wide recesses like hinge mortises; the ultra heavy duty tataki (right) excels at hand-chopping large mortises.

the bevel on stones is quick. And dispensing with the grinder simplifies the sharpening process.

If you use a mallet with your chisels, you might consider getting a Japanese hammer to use with these chisels. The hoop at the end of a Japanese bench chisel keeps the wood from splitting when it's struck with a metal chisel hammer. These hammers are lighter, smaller, and easier to control than large wooden mallets and deliver a more accurate blow.

Choosing a chisel

Although there's no real learning curve in using a Japanese chisel, it will have a subtly different heft and feel in use than a Western one. If you are new to these chisels, consider buying one in a size that you use often and working with it for a while to see how you like it. If you prefer it, I still wouldn't advise buying a full set unless cost is no object. You get almost no discount for buying a set of 10 and you pay a hefty premium for the larger sizes. Instead, I'd buy five or so in the sizes you use most. For me, that would be: 3mm (⅛ in.), 6mm (¼ in.), 9mm (⅜ in.), 12mm (½ in.), and something wide like 24mm (1 in.) or 36mm (1½ in.). Japanese chisels are usually sized metrically, and are slightly narrower than their imperial equivalents. The smaller widths—⅛ in. to ½ in.—are good for the relatively small dovetails I use on drawers. The ¼-in. and ½-in. chisels are also good for squaring mortises cut by machine. And having one or two wider chisels is nice for larger dovetails and larger mortises. All these chisels would work well for the various paring tasks that come up while making furniture.

Depending on need, you could fill out the set over time. Or use the money not spent on a complete set of bench chisels to buy some specialty chisels. Because hand-tool use is still a living part of the woodworking culture in Japan and because much of the woodworking there is highly specialized, there is a wide variety of chisel types.

You could get a wide shinogi-style push chisel, which is great for general-purpose paring (and not meant to be struck); a crankneck chisel with a short foot for cleaning the bottoms of dadoes; a heavy mortising chisel for hand-chopping large mortises; or a fishtail-shaped chisel, or bachi nomi, for working in tight spaces like the hard-to-clean rear corners of half-blind dovetails.

Steels and handles

The cutting edge of Japanese chisels is usually made from either "white steel," which is a very pure high-carbon steel, or "blue steel," which is white steel to which tungsten and

Specialty Chisels Abound

Japanese chisel makers still produce a wide array of specialty chisels for Japanese craftsmen plying traditional trades. Here are a few that are useful on the Western workbench. From left: a long shinogi push chisel for paring; a hiramachi chisel for access to tight spaces; a crankneck chisel for cleaning the bottoms of dadoes and sliding dovetails; a heavy mortise chisel for chopping mortises; and a very wide chisel for paring or chopping.

Fishtail chisel is worth reeling in. With its flared blade, the bachi nomi is superb for getting at otherwise inaccessible corners while paring.

Buying Guide

Japanese chisels fall into three general categories according to cost.

LOW END ($20–$40)

In this range, the maker's name will not be known—possibly because the tools are mass-produced. The handle may be dyed to mask inferior wood and may be poorly fitted to the ferrule. Blades may be stamped from sheet material and painted. Cutting steel may be soft and abrade away quickly. Hollows may be ill-formed. Blades won't get as sharp as better brands and will lose their edge more quickly.

MID RANGE ($60–$300)

Although made one at a time in small shops and typically attributed to a particular blacksmith, mid-range chisels offer the best value to furniture makers. Made with high-quality white or blue steel tempered to Rockwell c65 or higher, they should take a razor-sharp edge and hold it. Care in the making will be evident in the even shape of the hollow, a clean lamination line, a graceful transition from the neck to the body, and the fit of the handle to the ferrule.

HIGH END ($500 AND UP)

Some Japanese tools are treated as art, and with collectors in the picture, prices can get stratospheric. The provenance of a chisel—whether the blacksmith is a national figure—and features like folded-steel blades; exotic handles; and rustic, hammered surface treatments can increase the value of a chisel, but they don't improve its performance.

chromium have been added to make the steel tougher. The names white and blue steel have nothing to do with the color of the metals—they refer to the paper the steel comes wrapped in from the mill. There are different grades of both white and blue steel. White is said to take a sharper edge, and blue to hold it longer in use. In my experience, either kind can make an outstanding chisel. One of my favorite chisels is made with #1 white steel. It's easy to sharpen, holds a great edge, and is fairly durable. But I also have chisels made with blue steel that perform similarly. To me, the skill of the blacksmith is more important than the choice of steel.

Japanese chisel handles are often made from red or white oak, but boxwood, gumi, ebony, and rosewood handles are also fairly common. All except the ebony and rosewood are strong, tough, and resilient enough to make excellent handles. I find rosewood and ebony too brittle for chisels that will receive hammer blows, but they are fine for push chisels, which are meant only for paring.

A word about prices

Good Japanese chisels are not cheap. They start at about $70 apiece. But these tools are hand-forged by blacksmiths drawing on years and usually generations of experience

A Few Great Models to Start With

For workmanlike chisels of excellent quality, I suggest the Fujihiro brand (left in the photo), made by Chutaro Imai. "Workmanlike" is a compliment; these chisels are similar in quality to the ones I've been using for over 30 years. Made with white steel, they sharpen easily to a very durable edge. Well-crafted and finished, they come in the mentori profile and have red-oak handles and nice hoops. They are available with single or multiple hollows. A ½-in. (12mm) chisel is available from Hida Tool (www.hidatool.com) in Berkeley, Calif.

The next level of chisel, in my experience, takes an even sharper edge and holds it longer. An example is the Sekiryu brand (a 36mm Sekiryu is at center in the photo). These chisels are branded for Hiraide Tools (a large Japanese distributor), so the blacksmith's name is unknown. They are nicely made with an exceptionally clean back face, white-oak handles, and black finished metal with a kinari-style profile. They have wide side bevels for good access to tight spaces but are still robust enough for striking hard. Easily honed to a sharp and durable edge, a ½-in. (12mm) Sekiryu is available from Harrelson Stanley.

If price was no object, I'd buy all my chisels from father and son blacksmiths Akoi and Michio Tasai. At the very top of their craft, they make chisels in an array of finishes and styles (their shinogi paring chisel is at right in the photo). The standard Michio Tasai cabinetmaker's chisel, or oire nomi, with a mentori profile is beautifully made from yasuki, a type of blue steel, and has a black finish and red-oak handles. It will take an incredibly durable edge. This is about the highest level of chisel that I would actually use. A ½-in. (12mm) Tasai can be purchased at Tomohito Iida (www.japantool-iida.com), a wonderful Osaka dealer that carries many other fine tools.

who are at the top of their craft. They are using materials that are difficult to work and expensive. And they are creating arguably the finest tools of their kind. I'm constantly surprised that they don't cost more.

That said, in Japan there is definitely a level of "tools as art," and there are collectors around the world who buy them. It is not necessary—and it may be counterproductive—to go to that level to find a wonderful tool. For me, the most beautiful tools are those that perform their jobs the best.

Setting Up Your New Japanese Chisel

JOHN REED FOX

4 Steps to a Tuned-Up Tool

With its laminated blade and hooped handle, a Japanese chisel is built differently from its Western counterpart. And by tradition, a new Japanese chisel arrives with a fair amount of setup left to the individual craftsman.

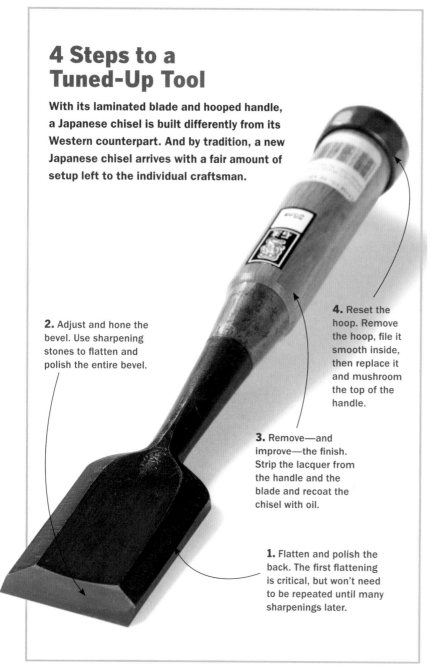

2. Adjust and hone the bevel. Use sharpening stones to flatten and polish the entire bevel.

4. Reset the hoop. Remove the hoop, file it smooth inside, then replace it and mushroom the top of the handle.

3. Remove—and improve—the finish. Strip the lacquer from the handle and the blade and recoat the chisel with oil.

1. Flatten and polish the back. The first flattening is critical, but won't need to be repeated until many sharpenings later.

Japanese chisels come in what Westerners might think of as rather unfinished condition. Setting the hoop, creating the appropriate bevel angle, and flattening the back of the blade are left to the craftsman. I also strip the finish from the handles and blades of new chisels and replace it with a coat of oil. (For the rest of the story on these unmatched tools, see "Choosing and Using Japanese Chisels," p. 67.)

Flatten the back

I begin setup by flattening the back of the blade. Unlike Western chisels, Japanese chisels have laminated blades: A thin layer of tough, high-carbon steel that can take a very sharp edge is fused to a thick layer of more malleable, shock-absorbing iron, which makes up most of the blade. The thin layer of steel on the back of the blade is the critical part of the tool, and it is hollowed out to facilitate flattening.

When flattening the back, the goal is to get the edges surrounding the hollow flat and highly polished. While the area along the front edge must be completely flat, it is not necessary to have 100% of the area up the sides perfect. Just flatten enough area so that the back will lie flat on your stones and will serve as a flat reference surface when you are using the chisel. I start on a 2,000-grit stone and proceed through the finer grits.

Once the back is flat, you will not have to repeat the flattening process until you have

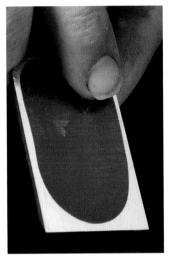

Flatten and polish the back. Holding the chisel perpendicular to the long axis of a 2,000-grit stone, apply medium pressure on the area just behind the bevel. It's essential that your sharpening stones are flat.

Make it flat around the hollow. The back of the blade is hollowed to make flattening easier. It's critical to flatten the front edge and most of the way up the sides, but not necessarily all the way up the back.

Work on the bevel. The bevel comes roughly prepared. But it needs help. Use sharpening stones—freehand (right) or with a honing guide— to adjust the bevel angle and flatten the bevel. To maintain a consistent stroke when freehand sharpening, be sure the chisel's handle is seated against your upper palm (above).

Check the new angle. Because the blade is mostly soft iron, altering the bevel angle on sharpening stones is fairly quick. Fox uses angle blocks to check that his new bevel is accurate.

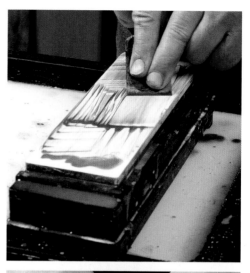

sharpened the bevel so many times that it threatens to intersect the hollow. At that point, using a coarse stone will effectively move the hollow up the blade. For day-to-day resharpening, you'll just hone the back with your finer stones. If you work the back regularly on coarse stones, you will eventually wear through the layer of high-carbon steel.

Hone the entire bevel. As you work through the finer grits, continue smoothing the whole bevel (top). A microbevel or hollow grind is not recommended on a laminated blade, as they reduce support for the brittle cutting edge. Hone the back with each grit (above) to remove the burr.

Create the bevel

With the back flat, it's on to the bevel, which comes roughly shaped. Because of their laminated construction, Japanese chisels should be sharpened to a flat bevel, never hollow ground. The thin layer of hard, brittle steel depends on the backing provided by the iron body of the chisel for support. Hollow grinding, especially on a small wheel, removes supporting material where it is most needed and may cause the edge to break.

Because most of the blade is made of relatively soft iron, the bevel can be adjusted

A good test for sharpness. You have a sharp chisel when you can make clean paring cuts in the end grain of softwood.

Prevent rust. Coat the blade immediately after sharpening with a rust preventer like camellia oil. You may find that a Japanese chisel's edge chips easily at first. This is because it is difficult to fully harden the very tip. After several sharpenings, you'll be into fully hardened steel.

Prep the handle. Use a flat-sided hammer to remove the hoop. If you are working on more than one chisel, keep track of which hoop belongs to which chisel. Then use lacquer thinner to strip the finish from the handle and blade. Use a scraper if needed to finish the job, then apply a coat of oil.

or honed quickly using sharpening stones only. I start with a 1,000-grit stone and make my way up through 5,000, 8,000, and 10,000. I find that for working domestic hardwoods, and even harder exotics like bubinga and rosewood, a bevel angle of 30° works well. If I am working soft woods like Alaskan cedar or Douglas fir, I might sharpen the bevel to 25° or 27°. The brittle cutting edge needs full support, so microbevels are not recommended either.

Set the hoop

The metal hoop encircling the end of a Japanese chisel acts as a retaining ring, enabling you to strike the chisel with a metal hammer without splitting the handle. Setting the hoop—adjusting its fit and

Fine-tuning the hoop. File away any burrs inside the hoop that might cut the handle's wood fibers. Then ease the inside edges at both ends of the hoop. The top edge should be a distinct chamfer, which will allow for a smooth mushrooming of the handle.

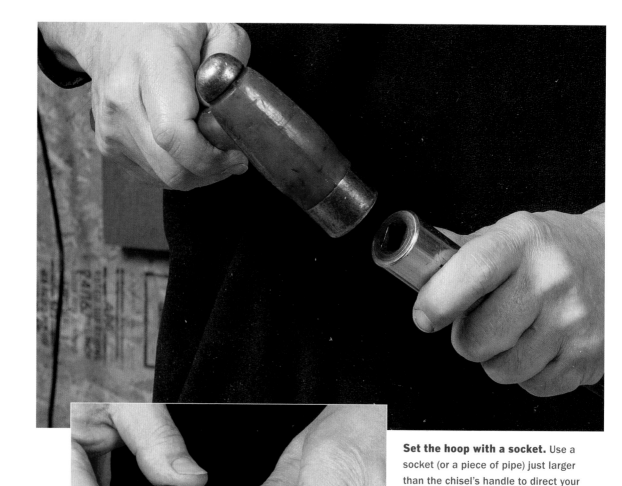

Set the hoop with a socket. Use a socket (or a piece of pipe) just larger than the chisel's handle to direct your hammer blows to the hoop. After the hoop is hammered down, about ¹⁄₁₆ in. of the handle should be showing above it.

mushrooming the wood to lock it in place—is another task left to the craftsman.

Start by removing the hoop. If it's tight, tap it off with a flat-sided hammer or a punch. If you want to remove the lacquer finish, this is the time to do it. I strip the handle and blade with lacquer thinner and wipe on a coat of camellia oil.

After smoothing the inside of the hoop with a round file and easing the chamfers on either end, test the fit to the handle. The inside of the hoop is slightly tapered to mate with the handle, so it will fit better one way than the other. It should be a very tight press-fit most of the way on but require a hammer to get it fully seated. In the end, you'll want ¹⁄₁₆ in. of the handle showing above the hoop.

If the hoop seats down too far on the handle, you can saw off the end of the handle, leaving ¹⁄₁₆ in. showing.

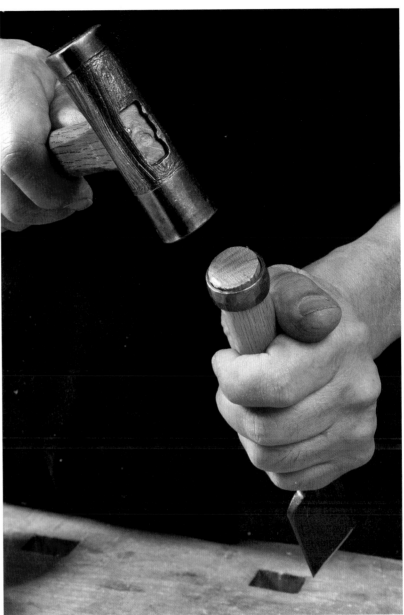

Drive it on by striking the hoop but not the handle (difficult), or by using a socket just larger than the handle to direct the blow (easy). Then, with the hoop seated, lightly hammer around the end of the handle to bend the wood fibers and lock the hoop in place. Using light strokes and a pulling motion, form a nicely mushroomed top and you're ready to put your new chisel to work.

Make a mushroom. Use light hammer taps with a pulling motion while gradually turning the chisel to create an even mushroom shape that will hold the hoop securely in place.

4 Must-Have Handsaws

MATTHEW KENNEY

I regularly use four handsaws in my shop, not because I'm a hand-tool nut but because a handsaw is often the smartest, most efficient choice for the job at hand. Take the job of crosscutting or mitering delicate moldings and miter keys. You could do those tasks at the tablesaw or miter saw, but you'd need to devise a jig to hold the workpiece during the cut, and there's no guarantee that the spinning blade won't chew up the workpiece. It's much quicker, safer, and cleaner to make the cut with a backsaw.

Handsaws are great for getting into tight spaces, too. A coping saw is the perfect tool to cut out the waste between dovetails. The thin blade can fit into even the tightest pin socket and make a turn along the baseline, removing the waste in seconds. Chopping out waste with a chisel takes much longer, and routing it out is possible only when there's enough clearance between the tails to fit the bit.

And then there are jobs that a power tool simply couldn't (or shouldn't) do, like cutting pegs flush. The only power-tool option is a router, and you have to make an auxiliary base to raise the router and then dial in the bit's cut depth so that it doesn't ruin the surface. Not to mention that pegs are often used on narrow parts, like legs, where the router can tip and ruin the part.

There are lots of handsaws out there, but I think the four you need most are a dovetail

Easy way to start the cut. After cutting a line with a knife or marking gauge, put the nail of your forefinger and thumb into it, place the dovetail saw's teeth against the nails, and push lightly.

Cut a clean shoulder. A crosscut backsaw is perfect for getting rid of the waste in the half sockets on the edges of a tail board. For the best results, chisel an angled groove along the scribed baseline (above) and use the vertical wall of the groove to get the saw started (left). The groove helps to start the saw in a straight cut, so that it naturally cuts down along the baseline, leaving no waste that needs paring.

saw, a backsaw set up for crosscuts, a dozuki, and a coping saw. I'll show you some tips on getting the best from each one.

Dovetail saw

I bought my dovetail saw to make hand-cut dovetails, but over the years I've found that it's good for other tasks, too, such as notching a shelf or drawer divider to fit in a stopped dado cut in a case side. For a smooth cut, I'd recommend a saw with about 19 teeth per inch (tpi), sharpened for a ripcut. Western-style saws cut on the push stroke and come with two different handle styles—pistol grip or straight. I prefer a pistol-grip handle, which makes it easier to push the saw and control the cut.

Crosscut saw

When you're making furniture, there are always small parts—like moldings, pulls, drawer stops, and pegs—that need to be cut to length. Instead of using a tablesaw, which could destroy those delicate parts in a flash, I use a Western-style carcass backsaw. A crosscut saw with about 12 tpi to 14 tpi and

A sawhook is great for small parts. The saw cuts on the push stroke, which helps keep the part against the fence while you cut. A large fence with two kerfs in it— one at 90° (above) and the other at 45° (left)—improves the accuracy of your cuts and prevents tearout. Locate the kerfs so that the fence will support a workpiece on either side of each one.

a blade that's a bit taller and longer than on a dovetail saw can easily make clean, accurate cuts in parts up to 1 in. thick and 3 in. to 4 in. wide. To increase accuracy, I use the saw with a sawhook, which is simply a flat board with a square fence (and a cleat that goes in your vise). The hook is great because it gives you a way to hold the workpiece still during the cut (both you and the saw press it against the fence) and helps to keep the saw cutting straight and square.

Dozuki

A dozuki saw has a thin, flexible blade, with fine teeth and a straight handle, which makes it well-suited to flush-cutting pegs. The flexible tip helps it get close to the base of a pin, and the straight handle is easier to hold and control with the saw on its side than a pistol grip would be. Get a crosscut dozuki with about 20 tpi. So why not just use a flush-cut saw? Their teeth have no set, so they clog and don't cut as well. Dozukis don't have those problems. The thin blade can kink, so get a saw with a replaceable blade.

Coping saw

With its thin blade and tall frame, the coping saw is adept at cutting curves. It was used in the past to cope molding to get perfect miters. But I use it when cutting dovetails. I was taught to chop out all of the waste with a chisel—a tedious job. When I tried sawing out the waste with a coping saw, it was a watershed moment for me, and I'll never go back. You don't need a super-expensive frame, but don't go with a hardware store cheapy, either. I spent about $20 on mine and it's easy to tighten and adjust the blade. The handle is comfortable, too. As for blades, get ones with a fine cut. They cut slower, which means the saw is less likely to jump the kerf at the end of the cut and damage the tail or pin.

Ride the spine. As you saw with a dozuki, press down on the spine to keep the teeth away from the surface. Use a chisel or block plane to flush the edging.

Sandpaper prevents scratches. Where the spine trick won't work, fold a small piece of sandpaper (abrasive side in) and put it under the blade to prevent the teeth from marring the wood.

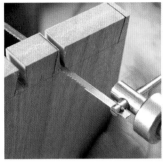

The teeth face the handle. This means the coping saw cuts on the pull stroke, which puts the thin, narrow blade under tension so it won't buckle.

One More Worth Having Around

If you've ever found yourself at the lumberyard with several boards that are too long for the bed of your truck, you'll appreciate having a panel saw. Carrying around a circular saw and hoping to find an outlet is more hassle than it's worth. But leaving a panel saw (8 tpi to 12 tpi) in the truck is no problem. Lay the boards in the bed with the gate down, and cut them to fit. I even use a panel saw in the shop to cut a board to rough length when it's too big for my chopsaw.

Get Sharp the Diamond Way

BRIAN BOGGS

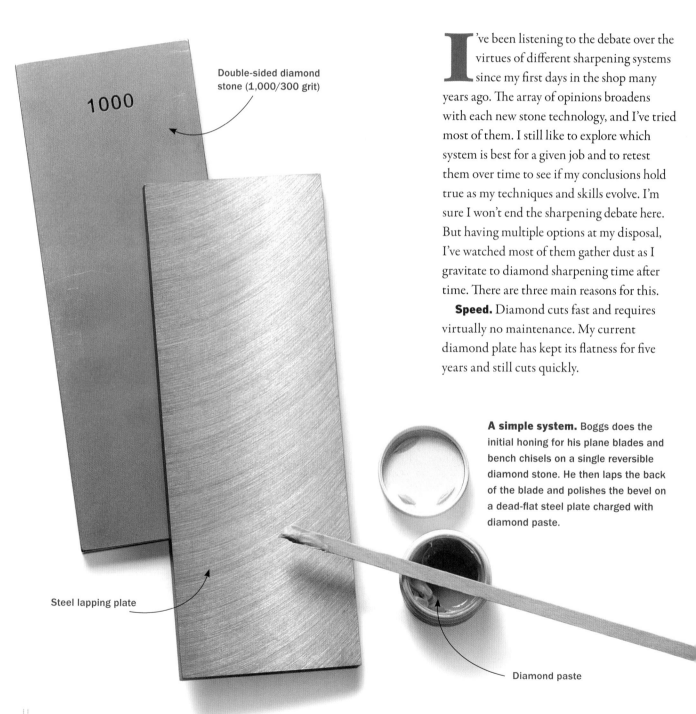

Double-sided diamond stone (1,000/300 grit)

1000

Steel lapping plate

Diamond paste

I've been listening to the debate over the virtues of different sharpening systems since my first days in the shop many years ago. The array of opinions broadens with each new stone technology, and I've tried most of them. I still like to explore which system is best for a given job and to retest them over time to see if my conclusions hold true as my techniques and skills evolve. I'm sure I won't end the sharpening debate here. But having multiple options at my disposal, I've watched most of them gather dust as I gravitate to diamond sharpening time after time. There are three main reasons for this.

Speed. Diamond cuts fast and requires virtually no maintenance. My current diamond plate has kept its flatness for five years and still cuts quickly.

A simple system. Boggs does the initial honing for his plane blades and bench chisels on a single reversible diamond stone. He then laps the back of the blade and polishes the bevel on a dead-flat steel plate charged with diamond paste.

Versatility. Diamond seems to sharpen every type of steel well, whereas softer abrasives like ceramic or waterstones don't perform as well on some of the alloys I sharpen, like A-2 steel, or on carbide.

Paste. Finally, diamond abrasive is available in paste form in a wide array of grits, allowing me to turn any piece of steel, aluminum, brass, or wood into a sharpening or honing tool (see "Diamond Paste Can Sharpen Any Shape," p. 88).

While diamond stones may cost more to buy than waterstones or oil stones, the process is quicker and the maintenance is nil. So I save time and money each time I sharpen.

Diamond stones and paste both use industrial diamond particles to do the cutting. In diamond stones, the particles are bonded to a metal substrate. In paste, they are suspended in oil. I've used a variety of diamond stones, but have settled on Trend® and Eze-Lap™ stones, which are both

excellent. I use paste from Beta Diamond Products (www.Betadiamond.com).

I sharpen in four stages: grinding, truing and sharpening, polishing, and stropping. After grinding the tool on an electric wheel, I create a bevel on a diamond stone. I polish the bevel and the back with diamond paste on a steel lapping plate, and I finish by stropping away the burr on a wooden block charged with paste.

Get sharp on a diamond stone

With a new diamond stone and a good grind on the blade, it should take only a few strokes to create an even bevel at the tip of the blade. The fewer strokes you take, the less likely you are to round the bevel and waste metal. I sharpen freehand, and I skew the blade as I push forward and back. If you use a honing guide, use your normal approach. Check your progress after the first few strokes. That might be enough to create the bevel.

Start on the stone. After hollow-grinding the tip of the blade, establish the bevel on the 300-grit diamond stone, a few strokes should do it. If you're doing just a touch-up, you can start on the 1,000-grit side of the stone.

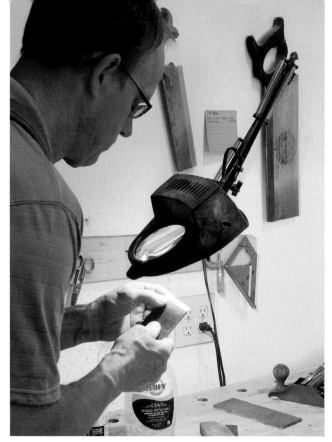

Let there be light—and magnification. A bright, even line at the tip of the hollow grind indicates accurate sharpening. When sharpening freehand, a parallel line will form at the heel of the grind (above). To monitor progress, a magnifying lamp is very helpful (left).

I typically start on a 300-grit stone and finish with 1,000-grit. But there are exceptions. If I am touching up a tool that doesn't need a lot of work, I go directly to a 1,000-grit stone. Also, newer stones will cut more aggressively, so if the 1,000-grit stone is new, I often skip the 300. I use a stone from Trend that has 300-grit on one side and 1,000-grit on the other.

You can use either oil or water as a lubricant. I use water with a little dish detergent in it. With oil, you need to clean your hands thoroughly after a sharpening session to avoid contaminating the wood.

When I am happy with the bevel's evenness and camber, I take it to a lapping plate charged with diamond paste.

Paste on the plate

For a long time I used an old Arkansas translucent stone for a honing/lapping plate, but I recently upgraded to a steel plate available from Lee Valley. Regardless of the

Polish with paste. Using a clean applicator, prepare for lapping and honing by spreading a BB-size amount of diamond paste on a dead-flat lapping plate.

Get the back flat. Boggs flattens the back of his blades on the lapping plate with 4-micron diamond paste and oil. After a new blade's initial flattening, it shouldn't require more maintenance to stay flat than the few strokes used to remove the burr during lapping.

TIP To get your lapping plate perfectly flat, rub it on 150-grit wet-or-dry sandpaper adhered to plate glass or a granite slab. Keep the glass or stone covered when not in use and reflatten the lapping plate periodically.

Brighten the bevel. A half-dozen strokes in 3-micron or 4-micron diamond paste on the lapping plate will bring the bevel to a high polish.

material your plate is made from, you will need a way to maintain its flatness. With a granite plate or a chunk of plate glass and some 150-grit wet-or-dry paper, you can sand any lapping plate to reasonable flatness. Use water as an adhesive and lubricant.

I tend to do all my lapping and stropping with 3-micron or 4-micron paste (roughly

Diamond Paste Can Sharpen Any Shape

You can easily create custom lapping blocks and use them with diamond paste to sharpen blades of nearly any shape. Boggs uses steel pipe, sanded smooth, to sharpen a gouge with a mating curve (below). He turns dowels to match other gouges. To sharpen his concave spokeshave blade (bottom), he made a lapping plate by doming the top of a wooden block.

Make a flat strop. Plane the top of a hard-maple scrap to prepare the surface for use as a stropping block.

Final polish and deburring. To cap off his regimen, Boggs strops the blade with 4-micron diamond paste lubricated with oil. The diamond particles become slightly embedded in the wood, producing a finer abrasion.

equivalent to a 4,000-grit stone). But if you use a variety of grits, you'll need a dedicated lapping plate for each grit. Diamond particles get stuck in the pores of the metal plate, so once you've used coarse paste, you have a coarse lapping plate. If you use a honing

guide, be sure to clean the wheels before honing and between grits.

Honing the bevel to a polish can be done quickly using diamond paste and WD-40® or 3-in-One® oil on your lapping plate. The paste is also available in a water-soluble version, but I use oil because it seems to cut better that way. You need only a tiny bit of paste—maybe the size of a BB—and a few drops of lubricant. I keep my paste in a jar and scoop out a dab with a fresh-cut piece of wood—or my fingertip, if it's very clean— and smear it around the surface of the plate. It's important not to let the diamond paste get contaminated, so I keep the jar closed. I also keep the plate covered between uses.

I find a lapping plate and 4-micron paste the best way to flatten the back of a blade. Stones always seem to produce a slight rounding. If the back of the blade has not been worked yet, I will spend a fair amount of time flattening it, but once it's flat I shouldn't ever need to reflatten it. Simply lapping it to remove the burr keeps the back of the blade nice and flat.

Strop for a high polish

As with any sharpening system, a burr is created as you hone each side of the blade, bending the fragile edge over to the unsupported side. Even though I go back and forth repeatedly on the lapping plate between the back and the bevel of the blade, I have never succeeded in completely removing the burr this way.

To finish the job—and to give the blade its final polish—I use a wood block charged with diamond paste. The diamond grit embeds itself more deeply into the wood block than in the steel lapping plate, making effectively a finer abrasive; the softer the wood, the deeper the diamond grains are embedded and the finer the abrasion. I typically use a block of hard maple.

Using this as a strop will polish the back and the bevel very well. I take a few strokes using my standard honing technique here. Then, to finally get the burr cleaned up, I push the tip of the blade through the end-grain corner of the block with a little added 4-micron diamond paste (see Tip at right).

If you already have a sharpening system that is working, then just add this wood strop and burr-removing trick and you'll enjoy better performance from your tools. If you aren't enjoying your sharpening tasks now, give diamonds a try.

TIP After charging the stropping block with paste, swipe the blade firmly through the end grain of the block 10 times or so to remove any remnants of a burr, creating an edge that takes silky shavings.

PART TWO

TECHNIQUES

Skill-Building Hand-Tool Exercises

JEFF MILLER

Before I made furniture for a living, I made music.

As a player in orchestras and brass ensembles, I stayed sharp in the way that most performers do, with hours and hours of practice.

So when I came into the woodshop, it seemed natural to practice my new skills with the same sort of discipline. Imagine my surprise when I found that practice is shunned by most woodworkers as much as it is embraced by musicians. But it's just as important.

Practice turns the tool into an extension of yourself. It builds and reinforces your muscle memory, letting you perform the physical tasks routinely and making them second nature. And that's key, because there's always more than just the physical task. You don't just saw or chisel—you need to do that to a line. Practicing lets you build up mastery of the underlying skills by isolating them—reducing them to basic elements of technique.

The exercises shown here will help. Work on them for 15 minutes a couple of times a week and your mastery and confidence will grow. Will they make you perfect? Nope. But they certainly will make you a better craftsman.

Saws

With proper technique, using any handsaw —western or Japanese—is a joy. The saw cuts easily without binding and follows a line without being steered. These exercises will help. Start with the right stance, with your forearm perfectly aligned with the back of the saw. To do this, stand slightly off to the side, with your hips at about 45° to the work. Your feet should be at least shoulder-width apart.

Saw without seeing

Clamp a ½-in.- to ¾-in.-thick board upright in a vise, with 5 in. or so above the jaws.

Eyes wide shut. Practicing with your eyes closed helps you focus on the sound and physical sensation of a smooth cut. Curl your fingertips under and let the saw brush the back of your index finger to help monitor the straightness of each stroke.

Practice sawing into the end grain with your eyes closed. This lets you concentrate on your mechanics, instead of watching the kerf. Make your grip light, as if you were holding a baby bird, and point your index finger forward along the blade. Try to generate all of the saw's movement from your shoulder.

With the cut under way, close your eyes and notice how the saw's action feels. How much pressure is needed in each direction for a smooth cut? Also listen to the sound of the saw as you cut. Strive for a very even sound throughout the stroke. A little of this practice goes a long way.

Saw to a line

The exercise of cutting one line without disturbing another helps develop your ability to cut accurately right next to a layout line.

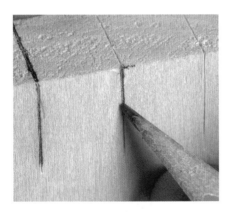

Saw to a line. Set a practice piece in the vise. Use a knife to make several clean lines about ¾ in. down the board and across the top. Now trace over these lines with a slightly dull pencil to create two pencil lines; one on each side of the incised line (left). The goal is to cut away one of the lines without disturbing the other one. Miller suggests beginning the cut with almost no pressure on the back of the saw. It may feel like you were actually lifting the saw off the work (center). A neatly sawn line leaves its twin undisturbed (right).

Handplanes

By practicing slowing down to plane, starting and stopping your plane, and planing a convex curve, you will develop the right stance and practice how to control and balance downward pressure on the plane.

Slow down. Pick a ¾-in.-thick board, at least 4 in. wide and 3 ft. or 4 ft. long, and set it up to plane on edge. With a smoother or jack plane, start at one end and move the plane extremely slowly (left). This makes it harder to plane incorrectly. Feel the push originating with your feet (right). Align your pushing arm in the direction of the cut and keep your wrist straight.

Start, stop, start, stop. Plane the entire edge again, but stop and start every 6 in. or so. Remember to maintain pressure with your hands (right) as you push all the way from your feet. With proper downward pressure, the cut will begin as soon as you restart. The goal is a continuous, unbroken shaving (far right).

Planing a convex curve. You should always plane "downhill" on a curve to follow the grain. But just for this exercise, try planing uphill, too. As you move the plane over the curve, balance downward pressure on the front and back to keep the iron in the cut.

Up to the line. Try to leave the scribed line perfectly straight without going over it.

Chisels

The following exercises are aimed at developing greater control over the chisel and a better understanding of how the chisel interacts with wood grain.

Pare to a line

Cut a rabbet on the end of a board. Then, with a marking gauge (or knife), scribe a line about ⅟₃₂ in. away from the rabbet. Use a ½-in. or ¾-in. chisel to pare to the scribed line. The goal is to leave the scribed line perfectly straight without going over it. This will teach you chisel control and how much you can pare away in a single cut without forcing the chisel backward.

Chase the line across. Once you're within $\frac{1}{32}$ in. or so of the line (closer is better for harder woods), start at one end with the chisel in the scribed line and pare down. Then move the chisel along the line, holding it so that about 80% is tight to the just-pared surface, with the rest in the line a little farther along. Pare and repeat all along the line.

Square up a hole

Squaring a hole will help you feel how the chisel interacts with wood grain. For control, hold the end of the tool like a pencil, with your hand resting on the work. Power the work with your weight and shoulder muscles.

Slice off a dowel

Drill a $\frac{3}{8}$-in. hole in a board. Next, pound in a dowel and trim it so that it sticks up about $\frac{1}{16}$ in. above the surface. Now use your chisel to pare the dowel flush. A slicing motion will help with this and is a useful technique to master. Push the chisel's edge sideways across the dowel with your guiding hand, while you push forward with the other hand on the handle.

Make it a square. Start with a scrap board at least $1\frac{1}{4}$ in. thick. Use a Forstner® or spade bit to drill a hole about $\frac{3}{4}$ in. deep and 1 in. to $1\frac{1}{2}$ in. dia. Now scribe a square tangent to the circle. Then pare the hole square.

Two directions at once. Move the cutting edge sideways as you push the chisel forward. This helps to trim the dowel flush without cutting into the board's surface.

Do More with Your Block Plane

JEFF MILLER

The block plane is a great acquisition for a woodworker of any skill level. Pound for pound (or ounce for ounce), it packs in more value than almost any other hand tool. The key is its compact size. A block plane fits in one hand, making it easy to control. It can be used with a delicate touch, and with your grip being so close to the wood's surface, it's easy to develop a good feel for the tool.

I'll show you how to use a block plane to take your woodworking to another level. But first, a few words about the tool itself.

Go low angle, and keep it sharp

There are two types of block planes, standard models with the blade, or iron, held at 20°, and low-angle models with the blade bedded at 12°, designed for end-grain work. Both types have the blade bedded with the bevel facing up. I would recommend a low-angle model as a first block plane. Get the blade razor sharp (I hone the bevel of the low-angle plane at roughly 30°), set up the plane to take fine cuts, and you'll get great results on end grain and long grain alike.

How to push (or pull) a block plane

The block plane is designed to be held easily in one hand, but I recommend using both when possible, to increase your control over the tool. There are a number of ways that I

Compact and Versatile

The block plane has no equal when it comes to trimming and refining furniture parts. It accommodates a variety of grips. Work one-handed to free up your other one to hold the work, or clamp down the workpiece and use two hands for more control.

Breaking edges

Trimming parts flush

Shaping and smoothing

Heavy planning is best done with the force coming from your lower body—all the way down to your feet—leaving your hands and lower arms for control. But for lighter cuts or awkward situations, you'll find that pushing with your arms is just fine.

A host of helpful tasks

One job where the block plane has no equal is bringing one part down level with another. Some woodworkers use a sanding block. But a sanding block is hard to control and can damage the surrounding surface. The block plane, on the other hand, is a precision instrument that lets you focus the cutting action where it belongs. Hold the work securely and work the plane with two hands, if possible, to better feel the surface below and do a better job of keeping the plane parallel to it.

Get everything level, and then use a sanding block for final smoothing.

Another task the block plane handles best is easing the edges of a project. Beginners often stumble at this stage, either sanding

Fast flush-trimming. The block plane is wonderful for bringing one part down perfectly flush to another and for leveling joinery, with no damage to the surface below. This makes it perfect for plugs and pegs. Whether it is plugs that cover screw holes or pegs used to strengthen mortise-and-tenon joints, the block plane brings them flush quickly. Angle the plane sideways as you push it forward, to make a cleaner, shearing cut.

add my second hand (see the photos on this page and the facing page); I even reverse hands and pull the tool through the cut when needed. It works just as well.

The cap at the back of the plane goes in the palm of your main hand, to help you push firmly. It also helps to keep your wrist straight so that your forearm lines up with the direction you want the tool to move. You want an easy and direct transfer of force from your body through your arm and the base of your hand to the tool.

Best way to trim edge-banding. Make solid-wood edging a little wider than the thickness of the plywood, and then plane it flush after the glue dries. To keep the plane level, run its heel end along the panel.

Great for dovetails, too. To avoid chipping off the edges of these end-grain dovetail pins, Miller planes in toward the drawer, where the grain is supported.

big, inconsistent roundovers onto the edges, or moving to the other extreme and leaving them too sharp. The block plane offers perfect control over the process, letting you do everything from a tiny chamfer to an obvious bevel or even a smooth roundover.

Working an edge can be done with either one or two hands on the plane, but if you are simply breaking the edges, the work goes faster if you hold the workpiece down with one hand, rather than clamping it in each new position. Hold the plane at 45° to the board, of course, but also skewed at an angle to the line of travel, ensuring that it will make a shearing cut for the smoothest results.

As with all handplaning, you want to cut with the grain, and you can usually

Level a drawer's edges. The block plane balances nicely on narrow surfaces, and can be held in a number of ways. Miller starts by planing down the highest edges (left). When they are level with the others, he changes his grip and pulls the plane around the corner (right) for a final clean pass.

determine its direction by looking at the predominant grain pattern at the edge. But the fact that you're planning at the intersection of two surfaces can make things tricky. You may have to simply check the results to see which direction works best.

If you're chamfering end-grain corners, as on the bottom of a leg or the ends of a panel, be sure to angle the plane so it is pointed toward the end grain. Otherwise, you will get tearout. To make a larger chamfer at any angle, you'll need to start with some basic layout. Mark out the final edges of the bevel on the two adjoining surfaces. Now take a guess at the angle to hold the plane and make a few passes. You'll soon be able to see how you're doing in relation to your marks and adjust the angle as necessary.

To ease an edge so it is even more pleasing to the touch, start with a 45° chamfer. Now

Quick roundovers. The nimble block plane balances nicely on corners, too, whether lightly breaking an edge or forming a full roundover. To make the corners of your projects softer to the touch, use the block plane to put a light, even chamfer on them.

Crisp bevels, too. To make perfect bevels of any size, such as on this tabletop, first lay out guidelines along the adjacent surfaces (above). Adjust the angle of the plane as you work toward the lines (right).

Change your approach on end grain. To avoid tearout when beveling the end of the tabletop, Miller points the toe of the plane toward the end grain as he planes. This shears it cleanly.

Detail work is no problem. A heavy bevel finishes off the bottoms of these table legs. Skew the plane for this end-grain cut, but make sure the toe starts out level for each pass.

plane the two corners to make an edge with three facets, and then repeat the process to achieve a roundover.

The block plane is also a good choice for smoothing gentle convex curves. You'll need both hands on the plane for this, and a bit of practice. Keep the plane aligned with the direction of cut and find the balance between your hands that brings the edge into contact with the work. Push forward with your lower body and concentrate on following the curve. This should feel like you were pushing the plane over a wheel that is rotating.

Great shaping tool, too. The versatile block plane can form everything from big curves to tiny facets, delivering glassy surfaces in seconds. Turn a bevel into a roundover by lightly planing the top corner (above left) and the lower corner (left) of a big bevel, and then making even lighter passes on the corners of the three smaller bevels. This will create a series of tiny facets that form a uniform radius.

Even it out. Light hand-sanding blends the tiny facets into one even roundover, faster than you could make it with a router, and cleaner, too.

Smoothing shallow curves. By rocking the plane forward as he goes, Miller is able to quickly smooth the bandsaw cuts on this table leg, leaving a more uniform curve than a sanding block would create.

The same feel and control over the plane's orientation makes the block plane wonderful for shaping and smoothing small parts, or small facets on larger parts. Check the surface as you go, adjusting your planning angle as needed, and then lock in the angle with your hands and arms and push with your upper body.

Forming small parts. After bandsawing this custom drawer pull, Miller cleans up each facet with the block plane. On a small surface, find the right planing angle, lock your arms, and push with your upper body.

Three Ways to Clamp a Drawer For Planing

MATTHEW KENNEY

Fitting a drawer to its pocket is a precision operation, which is why the handplane is the go-to tool for the job. With it you can remove material from the sides methodically to achieve a perfect fit. However, to take whisper-thin shavings from a drawer side, you need to secure the drawer in a bench vise. With traditional drawers, where the back is narrower than the front, that task can be tricky.

If the vise clamps only on the drawer front, the drawer really isn't stable enough to plane. If you clamp the drawer side between the

Why It's Hard to Plane a Drawer

If you clamp the side tightly between the vise jaw and the benchtop, you risk cracking the side at the drawer-bottom groove. But if you don't clamp it tightly enough, the drawer won't hold still.

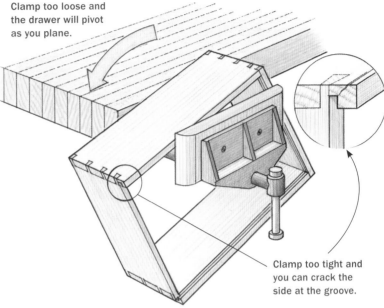

Clamp too loose and the drawer will pivot as you plane.

Clamp too tight and you can crack the side at the groove.

vise jaw and benchtop, you'll need a lot of pressure to hold the drawer steady enough for planing, and you run the risk of cracking the side at the bottom groove. However, if you back off on the clamping pressure, the drawer won't be supported enough and will pivot down as you plane it.

Fortunately, there are some simple ways to improve your vise's ability to clamp a drawer for planing, no matter what type of vise you have. The trick is to support the drawer from below. Doing so prevents it from pivoting down and allows you to grip the work with no danger of snapping the side.

A cast-iron vise attached to the front of the bench has a single screw and two guide posts to help control racking. Chris Gochnour uses those posts as a foundation for supporting the drawer. I use a twin-screw vise on my

Cast-Iron Vise: Use the Guide Posts

To hold a drawer in a cast-iron vise, place a scrap board on the guide posts. The board supports the drawer from underneath, allowing you to use less clamping pressure.

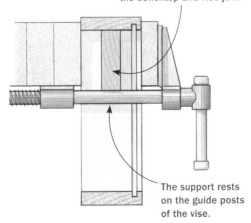

Size the support so the drawer sits just proud of the benchtop and vise jaw.

The support rests on the guide posts of the vise.

One support is enough. Make it ¾ in. to 1 in. thick, and short enough to fit inside the drawer. It should also be wide enough to project the drawer side slightly above the top of the jaw and benchtop but still low enough for clamping.

bench, and it doesn't have guide posts. To support the drawer from beneath, I pass two narrow pieces of hardwood under the drawer side. On one end the sticks rest on the benchtop, and on the other end they rest on the vise jaw.

Gochnour also has a great technique for a planing a drawer without a vise. Why would you want to do that? Well, if you have several drawers to fit—such as for a chest of drawers or jewelry cabinet—you can quickly move from one drawer to the next with this technique. It's just a matter of locking and unlocking a wedge between two supports. Using a vise, you would need to adjust the jaw when you switched between drawers of different height.

Clamp the drawer. Push down on the drawer as you tighten the vise (left). With solid contact between the drawer side and support board, the drawer won't give way under planing pressure (above). You can take confident and quick passes, fitting the drawer more quickly.

Twin-screw vise: Use two sticks. A twin-screw vise doesn't have guide posts, but you can use its thick jaw to your advantage. Place a pair of boards across the benchtop and vise jaw to provide a solid foundation for planing. The sticks run from the benchtop through the drawer, and onto the vise jaw (left). For big drawers, angle the sticks to get support under a larger area of the drawer side (right).

Clamp supports to the top. Align one support with the end of the bench. Place the second on the bench and slide the drawer over both. Push the second support against the back of the drawer and clamp one end to the bench.

You don't even need a vise. Use this trick when you need to plane graduated drawers in a case piece—they're the same depth but different heights. Rather than adjust a vise in and out to accommodate the height, use wedged supports to clamp the drawers.

Wedge the supports against the drawer. Slightly longer than the distance between the supports, the wedge forces them against the inside of the drawer.

Saw Like an Old Pro

CHRIS GOCHNOUR

There's no doubt that power tools like the tablesaw and router are efficient and put perfect joinery within the reach of even the newest woodworker. But that doesn't mean you don't need a backsaw. With a bit of practice a backsaw can become an extension of your arm, allowing you to make very accurate cuts quickly.

At that point, you'll find that there are times when a backsaw is actually a better option than a tablesaw or router, such as when you're building one piece of furniture rather than several identical pieces at once.

For a one-off table, you can cut tenons on the aprons with a backsaw as quickly as you can with a tablesaw, because you don't spend any time setting up the blade's height, positioning a stop on your miter gauge, or dialing in the settings on your tenoning jig.

A backsaw makes even better sense for difficult joinery like angled tenons, where a tablesaw and routing jigs would require too many fussy setups. And there are parts, like bed rails, that are just too big to tenon on a tablesaw. Also, don't forget that for many woodworkers, making furniture is as much about the journey as it is about the destination,

Your First Saw Should Be for Ripcuts

The best reason to get a backsaw is to cut dovetails and tenons by hand. Both involve a lot more cutting along the grain (ripcuts) than across it (crosscuts). So when you get your first saw, choose one that's sharpened for ripcuts. The secret to a great-cutting saw is a great sharpening job. That means a saw from the home center won't cut it. Instead, get one from one of the best saw manufacturers, who do this well. I've had good experiences with saws from Lie-Nielsen®, Veritas®, Bad Axe Tool Works™, Gramercy Tools®, and Wenzloff & Sons.

Ripsaws come in a variety of sizes. Don't get the dovetail size—they are too small for large dovetails in casework. Instead, get a carcase saw, which can handle tenons and case dovetails as well as dovetails for drawers and smaller items like boxes. Your first backsaw should be 11 in. to 12 in. long,

have 14 ppi (points per inch), and 2 in. to 2¼ in. of cutting depth beneath the spine. Don't worry about the crosscuts you'll have to make—a ripsaw works just fine for them. I've been using backsaws for decades and I don't own a crosscut saw. I've never had a problem with tearout or rough cuts. However, if you are willing to spend a bit more, there's a new type of saw that handles both rip- and crosscuts extremely well. The teeth have an old-school shape (called a "hybrid cut") that lets them cut across the grain just as well as along it. Both Gramercy and Bad Axe make this type of saw.

and hand tools connect them to the act of creating a piece of furniture in a way that is more fulfilling than using power tools. Making furniture (and not just the furniture itself) becomes part of the reward.

In any case, to get to the point where you can use a backsaw with efficiency and accuracy, you need to learn proper technique and then practice it. I'll demonstrate how to cut straight, which is the most important skill, and I'll show you some exercises to help you ingrain the correct mechanics in your body. I'll also give you some tips on sawing the two most common joints: dovetails and tenons.

One note before we get started. Although Japanese saws are wonderful tools, I prefer Western backsaws for joinery. I find their pistol grip and D-shape handles are more comfortable and make it easier to control the saw. Also, in my experience, Western saws are less prone to drift and deflect in use, because their blades are thicker and stiffer than those on Japanese saws, which are designed to be pulled rather than pushed.

Good posture is the key to cutting straight

Sawing well is an activity for your entire body, from your feet and legs to your arms

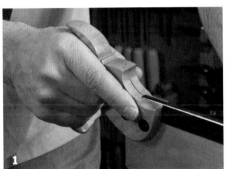

Start with proper posture. To saw straight lines, the tool must move back and forth in a straight path, like a piston. If you align your body with the saw, that straight cut happens naturally. Grip the handle lightly with three fingers, your index finger pointing forward and your thumb wrapped around the back of the handle (1). For righties, the left foot goes out front (2). For lefties, it's the opposite. And your legs should be slightly bent. Finally, think of the saw as an extension of your hand, with a straight line running along the spine and through your hand, wrist, forearm, elbow, and shoulder, so they all work in harmony (3).

and hands. So before you pick up a saw, take time to learn how to position your body. Your legs should be spread, one foot in front of the other, with knees slightly bent. Your torso should be turned, too, so that your arm can move forward and back in a straight line. If you have to swing your arm around your body, you cannot saw straight.

The distance between you and the workpiece is also critical. If you're too far away or too close, your arm will curve and your cuts will, too.

(Continued on p. 114)

TIP Hold it steady. It's difficult to saw fluidly and straight in a chattering board, a common event with cast-iron front vises, which clamp a board on only one edge. To eliminate vibration, clamp the board's other edge to the bench.

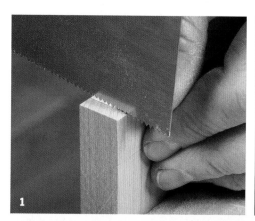

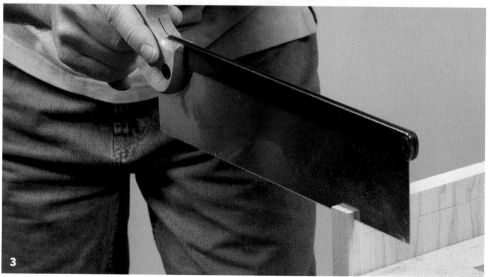

Learn to cut straight. The point of learning to saw is to cut joinery, but before you jump into dovetails or tenons, learn to cut a line straight and square to a board's face. That's the essential skill you'll need. Start on the far edge. Align the cut with your thumb (1). Without putting any weight on the saw, gently push it forward. It's easier to get just a few teeth started straight at the back edge than to get a straight start across the board's entire thickness. Lower the back of the saw as you cut deeper (2). After reaching the front edge, bring the saw horizontal (3) and cut down to depth.

Conquer dovetails one cut at a time. Repetition of good technique is the key to good joinery because it creates muscle memory. Don't worry about complete joints at first. Instead, spend time practicing the individual cuts that make up a tail and pin.

Tails

Practice should simulate the real thing. Lay out both sides of the tail on the same board. For the cuts right of center, always cut to the right (waste side) of the layout line as you would on real dovetails. On the left side, do the opposite.

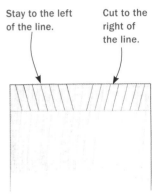

Stay to the left of the line.

Cut to the right of the line.

Pins

Same goes for pins. Lay out both angles on the same board and cut to the right of the line on the right half and the left of the line on the left half. Line up your body with the angled cuts.

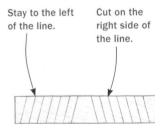

Stay to the left of the line.

Cut on the right side of the line.

Break down tenons, too.
Shoulder and cheek cuts are straight but big, and there's a strategy for handling each one. Shoulder cuts are first. The cheeks follow.

Practice the two basic cuts. It takes crosscuts and ripcuts to make a tenon. Practice them separately. Here's the drill for shoulders. Use a saw hook and your off hand to keep the board still. To get used to cutting down to a horizontal line, mark the depth on both edges.

Long cuts for cheeks. It's important that the depth of your test cuts replicate what you'll do for tenons, so they should be 1½ in. to 2 in. deep. Practice following the steps on pp. 114–115.

How to cut clean shoulders.
Shoulder cuts are tricky because aprons and rails can be several inches wide. It's hard to track a straight cut across that distance so make a track. After cutting your layout lines with a knife or marking gauge, use a chisel to create a V-groove along the shoulder line. You'll get a clean shoulder that will keep the saw cutting straight down.

Shoulder tracks the saw. Set the teeth in the V-groove, against the shoulder. Lower the blade until it rests in the groove across the board's entire width before you begin to cut.

Let the saw do the work.
There is no need to put any downward pressure on the saw. Its own weight is enough. The teeth will cut without any resistance or catching.

4 steps to great cheeks. This method lets you cut along just one layout line at a time, with each new cut guided by the previous one. To start make a shallow kerf, starting at the far corner. You'll use it as a guide to keep the saw straight as you continue.

Cut a shallow kerf along the top layout line.

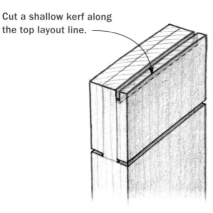

Work down the near edge. Angle the saw up and cut down the layout line closest to you.

Work down the front layout line without cutting down the back one.

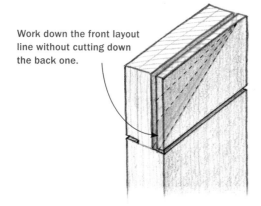

When you pick up the saw, hold it gently. And don't put any downward pressure on the saw as it cuts. A sharp saw—which yours should be—needs no more than its own weight to get the job done.

In addition to having the right body mechanics, you also need a bench that's rigid, so it doesn't flex or deflect under use. And it should be heavy or bolted down, so it doesn't skip over the floor. It needs a vise and a saw hook for holding parts. And don't forget to have good lighting around the bench so you can see what you're doing.

Cut down the other edge. Turn the board around in the vise and make another angled cut.

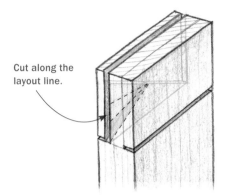

Cut along the layout line.

Level out and finish the job. All that's left now is a triangle of waste, but you have three straight kerfs to guide the saw as you cut down the middle.

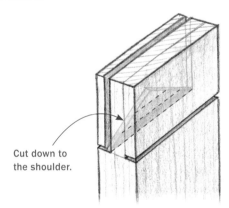

Cut down to the shoulder.

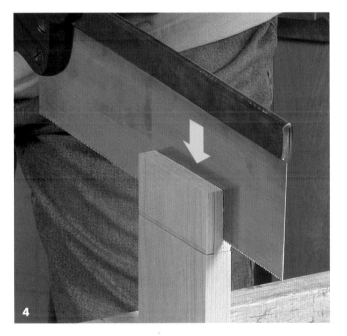

4 Chisel Tricks

PHILIP C. LOWE

It is often faster to make do with the tool in hand than to hunt for the perfect one and check that it is sharp and adjusted correctly. That's why I do so many things with a normal, flat bench chisel.

Just a handle and a blade, the chisel is an uncomplicated tool, but wonderfully versatile, capable of both rough and refined work. Chisels are also fast and efficient. I always have one or two within reach. Here is why.

Chamfer a tenon. Tenons fit into mortises more easily if their ends are chamfered. The quickest way to do that is with a chisel. Make sure to skew the blade. The lower effective cutting angle produces a smoother surface (facing page). Lowe typically skews the chisel 45° for most woods, but goes as high as 75° or 80° on difficult woods. As he reaches the end of the tenon (above), he pushes the chisel upward to cut with the grain and avoid tearout.

Pop a chamfer on the end. After placing the chisel edge on the narrow end of the tenon, a quick hit on the handle is all it takes to form the chamfer.

Trim a tenon. Lowe uses a chisel to quickly pare the cheeks and shoulders after sawing them close. The chisel's edge fits neatly into the scribed layout lines. The one on the edge controls the depth of cut and the one on the end grain keeps the chisel cutting straight, resulting in a tenon with parallel cheeks perpendicular to the shoulders. Work across the grain, because if you work with the grain, the chisel dives and rises with it and the cheek goes out of square. Later, when Lowe is ready to do the final fitting, he grabs his shoulder plane.

1. Quick chamfers

I chamfer the ends of tenons so they fit into their mortises more easily, and no tool does this faster than a chisel.

However, if you cut a 45° chamfer by pushing the chisel straight across the width of the tenon, you'll leave behind a rough surface and most likely will blow out the far edge. To avoid those problems, lower the handle of the chisel so that the cutting edge is skewed as it makes the cut. Then, as you reach the far edge of the tenon, slide the chisel up to cut with the grain rather than across it. That prevents tearout as the chisel leaves the cut. The edges of the tenon are a cinch. With the workpiece clamped vertically in a vise, come from beneath, so you're cutting with the grain. Skew the chisel slightly and give it a quick, firm pop with the palm of your hand.

2. Cut layout lines for precise paring

Nothing is faster at paring tenon cheeks and shoulders down to the layout lines than a chisel. From there, you can do the final fitting with a shoulder plane. Here's how I get it done.

First, I lay out the tenon with cutting tools: a marking knife for the shoulders and a cutting gauge for the cheeks. The crisp cut lines left behind in the wood become the perfect guides for your chisel.

The first cut takes you halfway. Stop there, so you don't blow out the other side.

The second cut finishes the job. Turn the workpiece around and come in from the other edge, meeting the first cut in the middle.

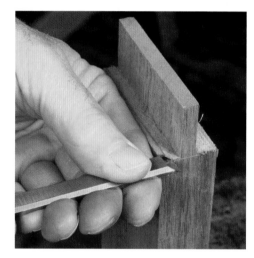

For shoulders, work perpendicular to the tenon. Put the chisel in the scribed shoulder line and start with a narrow cut, about ⅛ in. wide.

One cut guides the next. Place the flat chisel back on the first cut, at an angle to the face of the workpiece, and then straighten the chisel as you push the blade into the waste.

I remove the bulk of the waste with a saw, leaving about ¹⁄₃₂ in. for paring, so little that it won't force the chisel into the cheek or shoulder.

For the cheeks, I use the layout lines on the edges and end grain. The bevel goes into the line on the edge and is guided by the one on the end grain. I also use two cuts to pare a cheek, working from both edges into the middle to avoid blowing out the edge grain.

I've found it easier and more accurate to pare the shoulders if I work perpendicular to the tenon cheek. I start by paring just a narrow strip on the edge of the shoulder, about ⅛ in. wide. I then use that strip as a guide for my next cut by resting the corner of the bevel on it, which puts the chisel at an angle to the tenon. As I straighten the chisel, I push it into the cut and down to the tenon. I repeat that process across the width of the shoulder and end up with a shoulder that's even across its width and pared precisely to the layout line.

3. Angle the chisel to control chopping cuts

Mortising for a hinge involves two chisel techniques: paring and chopping. I lay out the mortise like I do a tenon, with a marking knife and cutting gauge, so I can use the layout lines to guide my chisel during paring. But first, I have to remove the waste from the mortise, which I do by chopping it with a bench chisel.

The hardest part of chopping is controlling how deeply the chisel cuts with every strike from a mallet. The best way to do that is by angling the chisel 45°. Here's how that works for a hinge mortise.

After laying out the mortise, I make a cut at both ends with the chisel perpendicular to the workpiece. Then, starting at one end, I make a series of "feather" cuts with the chisel angled at 45°. Angling the chisel prevents it from chasing the grain and cutting too deeply. Also, when the blade reaches the

TIP Angled tenons need a different approach. On the high side, cut across the grain to avoid tearout, but on the low side, pare toward the tenon.

Mortise a hinge. A hinge mortise needs to be a tight fit, but two chisels can handle the entire job quickly. For chopping, use one that is slightly wider than the mortise, and for paring, use one with a width that's less than the mortise's length. Remove most of the waste quickly—and in a controlled manner—with angled cuts, and then pare to the layout lines.

Get started with a perpendicular chop. Stay about 1/16 in. from each end of the layout lines.

Then work from an angle. Lowe holds the chisel at 45° with the bevel up. Strike the handle with a mallet, but use quick, controlled taps.

Clear the chips with a single swipe. Keep the chisel flat on the workpiece all the way through.

Clean up the bottom. Again, the scribe line is your friend. Put the bevel in the line and push in. Last, chop the ends right at the scribe line, and clean up those corners.

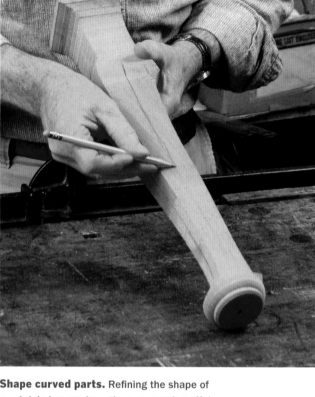

Shape curved parts. Refining the shape of a cabriole leg can be a time-consuming affair. Lowe speeds up the job by using a chisel to remove most of the waste. Start with layout lines. Lowe draws a centerline and two quarter lines on all four faces, so he'll know how much material to remove.

previous cut, it stops and won't cut any deeper. After reaching the other end of the mortise, I lay the chisel flat on the workpiece and pull it back across the cuts I've just made. Because the cuts were angled, there is very little material left holding the waste in place, and they come out easily. You're left with a mortise that is almost the exact depth required. To clean it up, just pare using the layout lines to guide the chisel.

4. Go bevel down on concave curves

As a period furniture maker, I've made a lot of cabriole legs. I've found that a chisel is the quickest way to go from the rough bandsawn shape to one that can be refined with a spokeshave.

As there are both concave and convex curves on a cabriole leg, there are two chisel techniques to use. For concave curves, use the chisel with the bevel down, so you follow its contours and keep the handle out of the way. Also, always work downhill, taking short "shoveling" cuts. That prevents the chisel from cutting too deeply and gives you better control.

Turn the chisel over, with the bevel up, for convex surfaces. By having the flat of the chisel on the work surface, you'll be able to cut facets as you work your way toward the rounded shape.

Go bevel down on concave surfaces. Like the short sole of a spokeshave, the bevel has no trouble following the curve.

Stay in control with short cuts. They prevent the chisel from cutting too deeply and causing tearout.

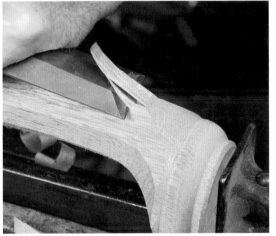

It's bevel up for convex curves. This enables you to make faceted cuts more easily.

File Joints for a Perfect Fit

CHRIS GOCHNOUR

Pick the right file. Gochnour prefers an 8-in. to 10-in.-long flat file with at least one safe edge. The cut of the file isn't critical, as long as it removes material with moderate speed and is easy to control. An 8-in. mill file (found at home centers as part of a set) is a good low-cost option. Gochnour's favorite joinery file is handmade in Japan.

No teeth on edge

The safe-edge advantage. To trim a dovetail pin or tenon, you must remove material from one part of the joint (the cheek, for example) without cutting into an adjacent surface (the shoulder). A safe edge makes this possible, because it has no teeth.

Fitting a joint is best done with hand tools, because they remove wood slowly and with great precision. This is why so many furniture makers have a shoulder plane or two in their tool cabinet. Chisels are another popular tool for fitting joinery.

However, there are times when you've trimmed to your layout lines and the joint still won't go together. At this point, a plane or chisel shaving would remove too much wood, leaving the joint gappy or loose. When the fitting gets that fine, I reach for a file to delicately trim the joint so that it slides together with hand pressure and closes up with no gaps.

Files are the perfect tool for this job because they remove material more slowly

Perfect for tenons. When a turned tenon is just a bit too big, a file with a safe edge is the best tool for trimming without damaging the shoulder.

than planes and chisels, affording you a great deal of control. You can target problem areas without turning a close fit into a bad one.

To hit the problem spots with the file, you must know where they are. Identify them with an old woodworking trick: Mark one side of the joint (tails, mortise) with pencil and then bring the joint together as far as you can with hand pressure. Take it apart. Look at the side that needs trimming (pins, tenon). Some areas will be marked with pencil where they rubbed against the mating part. This is where you file. If the joint still doesn't go together all the way, repeat the process until it does.

Gap-free dovetails. Pencil lead scribbled on the tails reveals where the pins need trimming. Line both sides of every tail with pencil. Several lines across the face are enough to get the job done. Knock the joint together, stopping when it begins to resist. Then pull the joint apart. High spots on the pins, which are keeping the joint from seating completely, will be marked with pencil lead. Use the file like an eraser, carefully removing the lead with a light touch. Repeat as needed until the joint comes together without gaps.

Hit the high spots. Extending your index finger over the handle helps the file cut in a straight line so that you don't round over the pin. Pinch the other end of the file between your fingers.

Friction-fit tenons. A mortise-and-tenon joint should go together with hand pressure, and it should not fall apart when one side of the joint hangs freely beneath the other. The controlled, fine cutting of a file is the perfect way to create this perfect fit. To prevent the file from tapering or rounding tenon cheeks, use your fingers to hold the file squarely against the cheek.

The best tool for double tenons. Two fingers on the file about 1½ in. from the leading edge keep it flat on the tenon.

Smooth Curves with Hand Tools

JEFF MILLER

When I started building furniture, my designs were simple, squarish Shaker and Mission-style pieces. But as my skills grew, I began drawing curves inspired by the human body, nature, or architecture. Curves became crucial to my work, making it more expressive, more appealing to the eye and hand.

Whether you bandsaw curves or template-rout them, they'll need smoothing afterward. Many woodworkers struggle with this and resort to sanding—dusty, tedious work that doesn't yield fair curves or crisp surfaces. I'll show you a better way to smooth both convex and concave curves using a handful of basic tools: handplane, spokeshave, rasp, and scraper. You'll get smooth curves without kinks, flat spots, or bumps—surfaces that invite hands to run along the edges of your work.

Bear in mind that these tools are for flat (so to speak) edges, as opposed to sculpting freeform, rounded shapes.

Curves of Every Style

Every furniture style has its own visual language, and the vocabulary usually includes curves. Prime examples are the formal legs on a traditional Shaker stand, the scrolled base on Alan Turner's period dresser, and the restrained arcs on Chris Gochnour's contemporary desk or the author's modern chair.

Bases

Legs

Drawers

Chairs

A Compass Plane Is a Curve Specialist

If you do curved work often, consider getting a compass plane. Its flexible sole adjusts to a range of curves. A few companies make new models, but an old Stanley 113 is fairly easy to find and is still the best.

Handplanes can handle some curves

For gentle-to-moderate convex curves (or very gentle concave ones), I start with a sharp handplane set up for a light cut. A plane chatters less and smooths more efficiently than lighter tools.

With a bench plane, I use a standard grip on the handle and tote. I also hold a block plane with two hands. On convex curves, very little of the sole rides the surface, so control the tool by balancing downward pressure, fore and aft, to keep the edge in the cut. Two things help: First, power the stroke with your lower body, not your arms. Second, roll the plane forward as you move, as if you were pushing it around a large wheel. On concave curves, skew the tool to shorten its sole. With any curve, if you can't follow the curve with a plane, it's time to switch tools.

Essential Kit for Curves

You can smooth curves quickly with just a bench or block plane, a spokeshave, a rasp, and a scraper. Miller keeps them all handy, and starts with the largest tool that can handle the curve. Mass equals momentum.

BLOCK OR BENCH PLANE

The popular No. 4 smoother (top) works well; a smaller bench plane perhaps a little better (Miller often uses a No. 2). Most versatile is a high-quality block plane (bottom). Miller says it doesn't need an adjustable throat opening or a low angle. Just sharpen the blade and set it for a light cut.

SPOKESHAVE

The shave's short sole lets it smooth hollows that a longer tool would bridge over. A flat-soled shave works well on steep convex curves and moderate concave ones. A convex sole reaches into tighter concave curves, but is harder to control.

RASPS

The rasp fits where edge tools won't. Miller uses a fine-grain Auriou™ (their No. 13) but has a coarser rasp (a No. 9 or No. 10) for heavier stock removal. There are even coarser models, but they are for 3-D shaping and rounding.

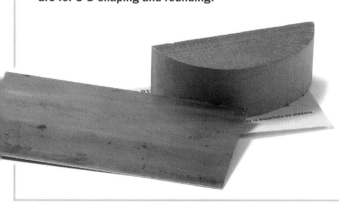

SCRAPER/SANDING BLOCK

Use a card scraper or sanding block on tearout-prone areas where grain changes direction, or for smoothing spots that have already been worked by the other tools. Set up the scraper with a light to moderate burr.

Convex curves. Miller likes to start with the largest plane that can navigate the curve. A heavier tool will chatter less and leave a smoother surface, but its longer sole requires more finesse to control.

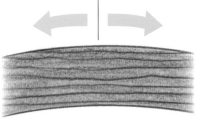

To minimize tearout with edge tools, work in the direction of the emerging grain. Read the grain on the side of the piece to orient the work. Most often, you will find yourself planing "downhill" from the crest of a convex curve.

Plane with the grain. Hold a block plane with a forefinger on the front knob and the opposite hand wrapped around the front to apply downward pressure as you move forward.

Shaves work curves, inside and out

Spokeshaves are made to smooth curves, both convex and concave. The short sole makes it easier to follow a curve, especially when the radius is tight or changing.

Hold the tool with your thumbs pushing on or near the blade and your fingertips at

Spokeshave for tighter curves. A spokeshave handles steep curves more nimbly than a handplane. Control the shave with your thumbs on the back edge of the blade or the shave's body. Your index fingers regulate downward force on the front of the tool.

TIP Watch the line. To avoid beveling the edge, use the bandsaw marks to track your progress. Try to remove them evenly as you go. Once they're gone, switch to a square as a final check.

Concave curves. Start with a spokeshave. With its minimal sole, a spokeshave can settle into concave curves that are too deep for a handplane to fathom.

the front. This lets you vary the angle of attack to follow the curve as you push with your lower body. The shave has very little mass to dampen vibration, so work slowly to avoid chatter. A sharp blade is crucial.

Skewing the tool lengthens the sole on the surface, reducing chatter, bridging high spots, and making it easier to start a cut. Be careful not to bevel the surface sideways, though. Check it periodically with a square.

To avoid tearout where the grain changes direction at the bottom of a concave curve, try rolling the tool back so that the edge stops cutting as you approach the bottom. Finish those transition areas with a scraper or sanding block to remove any tearout.

Work Downhill

On a concave edge, the grain will typically change direction at the bottom of the valley.

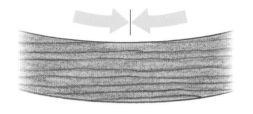

Scrape or sand the transitions. After working the surface with edge tools and a sanding block, use a card scraper to remove any tool marks and refine the surface, especially in tearout-prone transition areas.

Smooth the edges. Most curved edges can be smoothed with a sanding block shaped to fit the workpiece. It's great for tight curves or where grain direction changes. Start with P150 grit.

Keep a rasp ready

On some curves, the radius is too tight, the curve dies into a corner, or the surface just can't be reached with an edge tool. A rasp's half-round face is ideal for tight inside curves and its cutting action lets you approach the work from any angle. Hold it by the wooden handle (a must) with the other hand guiding lightly at the tip. A well-sawn curve needs only a light touch with a fine rasp, but the surface will be rougher than one left by a plane or spokeshave. Follow with a scraper or sanding block.

Very tight curves? Use a rasp and two hands. Angle the rasp slightly, push forward (rasps do not cut on the pull stroke), and lift at the end of the stroke.

Remove the rasp marks. The surface left by a relatively fine-grain, higher quality rasp is easily cleaned up with a scraper.

Sand for consistency. After smoothing with edge tools, you may want to give the entire edge a light sanding with P220 grit to achieve a consistent surface.

Make the Spokeshave Your Secret Weapon

CHRIS GOCHNOUR

When it comes to refining curves and shaping contoured work, there's nothing better than a spokeshave. Mechanically, a spokeshave works the same way as a handplane, but its small sole makes it ideally suited for following curves. After you've cut out your work on the bandsaw or router, a spokeshave steps in to remove sawmarks and irregularities with precise fingertip control.

Spokeshaves come in a wide array of styles and designs (see "Specialty Shaves," p. 138). The most versatile and perhaps the easiest to start out with is a standard-angle shave, with a flat sole and the blade mounted bevel down. This type of shave can handle most of the curves—concave and convex—a furniture maker will encounter. Here I'll show you how to get the most out of this special tool, from setup to shaping.

Set up for success. The first shave to buy is a flat-sole, bevel-down version. It can negotiate all but the tightest curves, and in most situations it leaves a smooth finish without tearout.

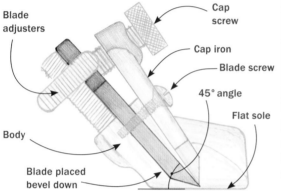

Cap screw

Cap iron

Blade screw

45° angle

Flat sole

Blade adjusters

Body

Blade placed bevel down

Insert the blade and put on the cap. Make sure the bevel is oriented correctly (down, in this case) and that it rests flat against the bed. Slip the cap iron into place and tighten the cap screw—enough to hold the blade securely, but still allow you to adjust it.

Install and adjust the blade

As with a bench plane, the first step with a spokeshave is to sharpen the blade. Because of its small size, sharpening can be tough, but I have a jig that takes the pain out of the job. Once sharp, it's pretty easy to install and adjust the blade for perfect results.

Most newer spokeshaves have twin adjustment screws that move the blade laterally as well as in and out, making it easy to get the blade in the proper alignment. With the blade drawn into the body, begin by tightening the cap screw (or screws) to hold the blade. Slowly rotate the adjusting screws to advance the blade and stop when the blade begins to project proud of the sole. You can sight along the shave's sole for the initial setup, then try out the shave on a wood scrap and adjust the blade until you get the right setting. It's best to start with a light

Adjust the blade. Sight along the sole and raise the blade until it begins to project and is parallel across the sole. Test it on a scrap and fine-tune the setup as needed.

cut, and advance the blade as needed. For an even-depth cut, the blade should project evenly and be parallel to the sole. Check it by taking a shaving with each edge of the blade—it should cut the same on each side.

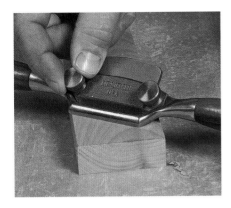

No Adjusters? No problem. Some shaves don't have adjustment screws, but the setup is just as fast. Place the shave on a block of wood, insert the blade until it touches the wood, then tighten the screws.

Then tap it out. A few taps with a small hammer on the back of the blade gets it into position. For lateral adjustments, tap on the side of the blade.

Back out the blade for fine cuts. The easiest way to do this is to flip over the spokeshave and tap it against the bench.

If your shave doesn't have adjustment screws, don't worry. Loosen the cap screws and set the shave on a flat piece of wood. Insert the blade until it touches the wood, then tighten the screws. Test it out first—it should make a very light shaving. If you need a deeper cut, advance the blade with a few light taps on the back with a small hammer. Tapping in the center moves the blade forward, and tapping the sides moves it laterally. To back out the blade for a

Concave Curves

Start at the ends and shave downhill toward the center, working with the grain.

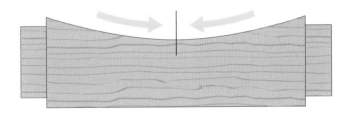

Grip it and rip it. Use your thumbs to push the shave (left), gripping both handles between your thumb and index fingers and wrapping your other fingers around the handles. For a pull cut (right), turn the shave around and hold it the same way, but pull with your index fingers.

Avoiding tearout trouble. Watch out for reversing grain. If you notice tearout or feel the blade digging in, try cutting from the other direction. This tearout (above) is from cutting uphill in white oak. The best way to check for bumps and tearout is to run your fingers down the edge (right). They'll feel bumps you can't see.

Convex Curves

Start the shave at the top of the curve and work downhill with the grain.

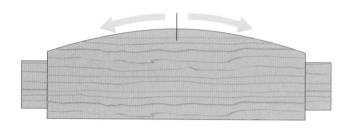

Start high and work low. Gochnour starts in the center and pushes toward the low end of the curve (above). To smooth the other side of the curve, he reverses his grip and pulls the shave, always cutting with the grain (left).

Extra steps for wide stock. Work wide curves evenly. Gochnour works systematically to create an even surface on this drawer front—watching the bandsaw lines to keep him on track. This works well on narrow edges, too.

shallower cut, hold the shave upside down and gently tap the handle on the bench. Be careful of tapping too hard—if it takes more than a few light taps, it's better to loosen the cap screws and pull the blade in, then advance the blade out again with a hammer.

For best results, cut with the grain

Spokeshaves excel at smoothing out bumps and refining curves fresh off the bandsaw. To give you the basics, I'll show you how to refine the concave and convex curves of an arched table apron.

The main idea is to cut with the grain, or downhill. On the concave edge, start at one end and cut downhill until you reach the low point of the curve. Do the same for the other side, always shaving downhill toward the center. If the wood tears out or the tool digs in, stop and check the grain direction—you may need to reverse your approach.

Because of its short sole, getting the shave started isn't always easy. But there's a trick for

Skew the shave for an easier start. When it's tough to get the shave started, try holding it diagonally to the work. It makes the sole longer, so it's easier to smooth out those first few high spots.

Profile an Edge

1. Draw the profile.

2. Mark and cut 45° bevels.

3. Remove the peaks and finish shaping.

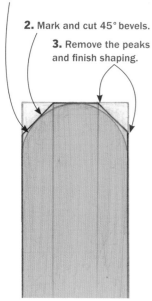

Bullnose starts with a bevel. Use a combination square to mark guide lines for the profile (above left). Shave to the lines to create 45° bevels, then do it again to create 22.5° corners (above right). Set the shave for a lighter cut, and smooth away the remaining facets (right).

that: Skew the shave by holding it diagonal to the workpiece. This lengthens the sole, giving you more support for a smoother start. After the rough sawmarks and major bumps are beginning to smooth out, go back to a normal grip and clean up the rest of the arc with a few more passes.

To remove stock evenly and maintain a flat, square workpiece, watch the sawmarks—you want them to disappear evenly on each side. Keep working until the sawmarks are gone, then check your progress against the layout lines. Your hands often can feel differences that your eyes can't see, so to find those last bumps and dips, try running a hand along the curve.

Once the concave side is finished, flip the workpiece over and begin smoothing the convex edge. The principle is the same. Start the shave at the highest point of the arc and work downhill with the grain.

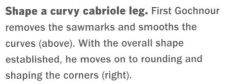

Shape a curvy cabriole leg. First Gochnour removes the sawmarks and smooths the curves (above). With the overall shape established, he moves on to rounding and shaping the corners (right).

Broader curves, such as on drawer fronts, can be handled the same way. Just like before, rotate or skew the shave to get it started in rough spots and straighten it as the surface begins to smooth out.

Rounding an edge. You can round curved edges, too, like the bullnose edge profile of a curved tabletop. Cut out the curved edge and smooth it with a shave. Lay out some pencil lines for the bullnose profile, starting with a 45° bevel, then set the shave for a deep cut. Shape the 45° bevel first, then knock off the corners with 22.5° cuts. Finally, reset the blade for a light cut to make it even smoother. You can leave the last small facets if you like or sand the profile smooth.

Shaping a cabriole leg. The flowing curves of a cabriole leg really show off the strengths of this tool. When all of the bandsaw marks are removed and the curves of the leg are smooth, begin to round the corners of the leg. The corners of cabriole legs transition gradually from square to round, so mark sets of lines down the corners to give you a guide. Set the shave for a deep cut and rough the leg to shape. Work with the grain, switching directions if necessary. For the final smoothing, set the shave for a fine cut and rotate the shave slightly with each cut. Smooth out any remaining tiny facets with sandpaper.

Specialty Shaves

For extreme curves and tough end grain, a specialty shave can save you time and give superior results.

LOW-ANGLE BLADE FOR END GRAIN

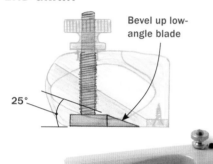

Bevel up low-angle blade

25°

Bevel-up shaves are the traditional choice for shaping green Windsor chair spindles, because the low cutting angle follows the grain nicely. They handle end grain better than a standard-angle shave, too, leaving it super smooth.

ROUND SOLE FOR TIGHT CURVES

Convex curved sole

Reach for a round-sole spokeshave to refine tight, concave curves, like the ones on this cabriole leg.

CONCAVE SOLE FOR SHAPED PROFILES

Blade and shave have matching curved shape.

This shave's concave bottom won't leave flat facets on rounded profiles like the one on this tabletop, and it's great for round chair spindles, too.

Create Your Own Scratch Stocks

GARRETT HACK

Every so often you discover a hand tool that changes your woodworking. Scratch stocks have changed mine. These versatile tools have not only greatly expanded my ability to create fine details, but they've also changed my design aesthetic, allowing me to play with edges to create custom profiles that fit perfectly with my work. And the design possibilities are almost limitless.

I use a shopmade scratch stock. It's really just a small metal scraper sharpened to carve a detail into an edge and held in a block of hardwood. You can make any shape you want way beyond what any stock router bit can achieve. I use them to cut finely molded details like delicate beads as well as perfectly excavated inlay grooves. Well-sharpened, a scratch stock will cut cleanly in any wood, even in the most ornery or figured species.

Here I'll show you how to make a simple scratch stock and give you some tips on using one. This size works for many applications. It will cut as far as 1 in. from the edge. For cuts farther in, you'll need a larger blade and/or holder.

Shape the scraper. Cut out the scraper blank from a piece of spring temper steel. Hack takes it from an old handsaw blade. The size will vary based on the profile you're trying to achieve, but for a simple bead a blank 1 in. by 1¼ in. is good.

Smooth. Use a flat mill file to square up the edges. Hack holds the scraper in a small machinist vise but lacking that, you can use a bench vise.

Shape. A bead profile is a great starting point for getting into scratch stocks. To create the profile Hack uses a round chainsaw file.

Create the profile

The best steel to use is the kind found in an old handsaw or card scraper, known as "spring temper" steel. It's soft enough to take a profile easily yet durable enough to hold an edge in almost any wood.

I start by cutting a blank that's roughly 1 in. by 1¼ in. Use a flat file to square up any edges of the blank that you'll use. Once that's done, it's time to create the profile, in this case a simple bead. I work by eye, but for your first time you may want to draw it out on the blank. Your call. A blank can have four different profiles, if you'd like—one on each corner. Then you simply rotate the scraper in the holder to the profile you want to use.

Holding a round file horizontally and just in from the corner of the blank, cut until it is about half buried in the edge. The shape can be round or oval. The goal is to leave a small tooth on the corner. That tooth cuts the groove, or quirk, that defines the bead. A fine tooth works best. Once the profile is created, it's time to sharpen.

Hone the edges

Each profile has two cutting edges, which means you can cut both forward and backward. And that's part of the reason a scratch stock can cut so cleanly, because you can always cut with the grain no matter how it changes.

Both of those cutting edges must be honed square and polished. Right off the file, a scratch stock cutter will do serviceable work, but honing the edges will make it operate far better. I start with a coarse stone, 600 grit to 1,000 grit, to remove any file marks and surface corrosion on the steel.

On the faces, you don't have to hone the entire scraper, just the area around the profile. For the bead profile, hone the top of the tooth, the two faces of the scraper, and the outside (and original edge of the corner). For the concave areas of the profile I use slip stones. If you don't have slip stones, shape a piece of hardwood and wrap it with fine sandpaper or smear it with a bit of diamond paste to work the concave areas. Work up through the grits. I often hone an edge to 8,000 grit, but you can stop well short of this. The advantage of honing more is that the edge will be sharper and last far longer.

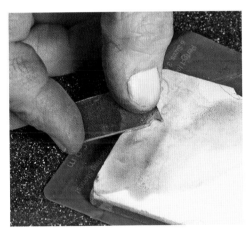 

Get it sharp. Hone both faces of the scraper (left), working through the grits from coarse to fine. You have to polish only the area immediately around the cutting profile. Finally, hone the edge of the scraper to a nice polish (right).

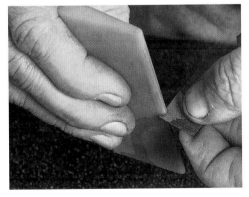 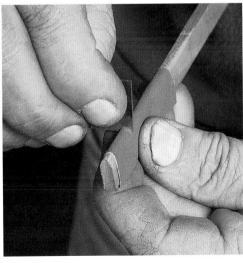

Get inside. To hone the concave area of the scraper, Hack uses a slip stone (above). You can substitute a rounded stick or dowel and fine sandpaper (right) to do the same job.

Add a holder. Size the holder to fit your grip—⅞ in. thick by 1¼ in. wide by 3½ in. long is a good starting point. Smooth its surfaces and chamfer the edges, then cut a kerf for the scraper.

Add a Holder

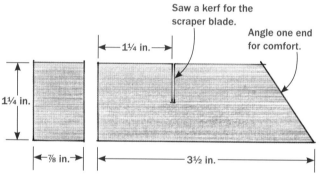

Saw a kerf for the scraper blade.

Angle one end for comfort.

1¼ in.

1¼ in.

⅞ in.

3½ in.

Make the holder

Once the scraper is ready, make a holder. Generally, ⅞ in. thick by 1¼ in. wide by 3 in. long is a good size, but size the block to fit your grip. I use a hardwood scrap, smoothing the surfaces and breaking the corners with a block plane so it is comfortable to hold.

Saw a kerf at right angles to the length of the stock and cut about halfway through.

Install the scraper. Tap in the scraper until it bottoms out in the kerf (top). Then adjust its projection (above) from the block to locate the bead (or other profile) perfectly on the work. Test it on scrap until you have the location nailed.

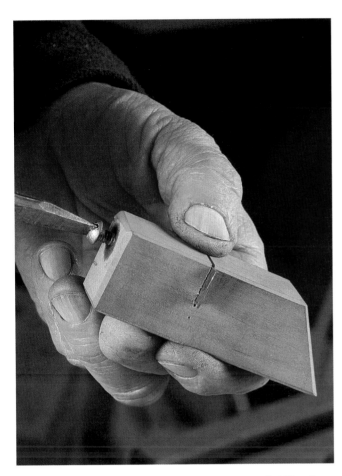

Cure for a fat kerf. If the scraper is loose in the kerf, drill and install a screw or bolt to wedge it in place.

Use a saw that has a slightly smaller kerf than the steel you use for the scraper. With a hammer, tap the scraper into the holder. Then position the scraper horizontally until it cuts exactly where you want it to. Test the setup on scrap until you're dialed in. The fit should be snug enough that the blade remains fixed in use. If the kerf is too wide for the scraper, put a machine screw into one end of the holder and tighten it against the scraper. Now you're ready to cut.

Tips for using any scratch stock

I have dozens of scratch stocks with different profiles. Whenever I want a new edge detail, I just make a new scraper or file the profile into an existing scraper. No matter the profile, they all cut the same way. Here are some keys to success.

In general, these are scraping tools, and they don't cut a lot of wood quickly. Let them cut. Light pressure is best. Angle the scratch stock forward when pushing it. Angle it backward when pulling. The harder the wood the better the results you'll get, especially for very fine profiles. Ebony is wonderful; so are maple and rosewood.

I like to cut repeatedly in the same direction for a half dozen strokes, then reverse. One direction always seems to work more smoothly, and that's the direction I typically finish with. Since these scrape, you'll end up with a surface that's pretty smooth, but I like to finish them with some very fine sanding, 220 grit to 320 grit.

Give scratch stocks a try. You'll quickly see a big difference in your furniture.

How It Works

There's really no limit to the profiles you can create with a scratch stock. The two that Hack uses most often are for beading an edge and excavating for string inlay. Regardless of the job, the technique is the same. For best results, use a light touch and angle the scraper in the direction of the stroke.

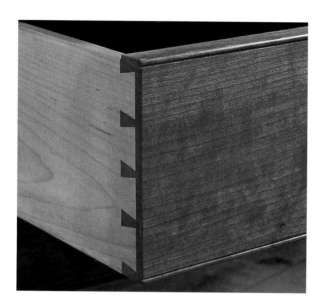

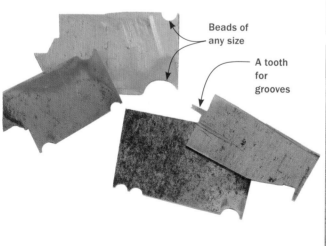

Beads of any size

A tooth for grooves

BEAD WITH A QUIRK

Colored pencil guides the way. Mark the apex of the bead (or the high point of a different profile) on the edge of the board (above left) and adjust the scraper so that its tooth is just beyond that mark (above right). Cut until the pencil line just disappears (left). This will create a bead that's parallel to the original surface. Remove any fuzz with fine sandpaper (below).

APPLIED BEAD

A standout detail. To make applied cock beading for a drawer, door, or apron, Hack uses the scratch stock to round over the edge of the thin workpiece. Again, he takes light passes in both directions.

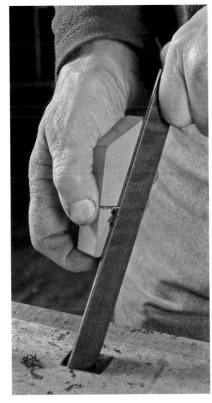

GROOVES FOR STRINGING

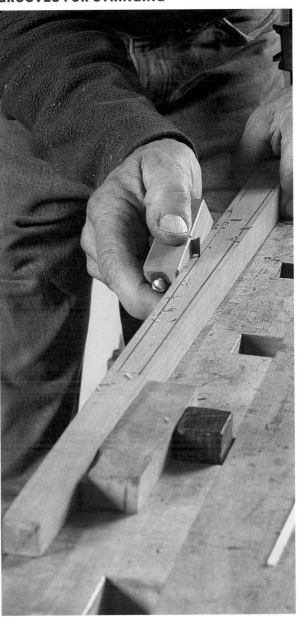

Works as an inlay tool. Hack uses scratch stocks to excavate for string inlay. The scraper is filed with a tooth profile to match the width of the stringing.

Make Custom Moldings

GARRETT HACK

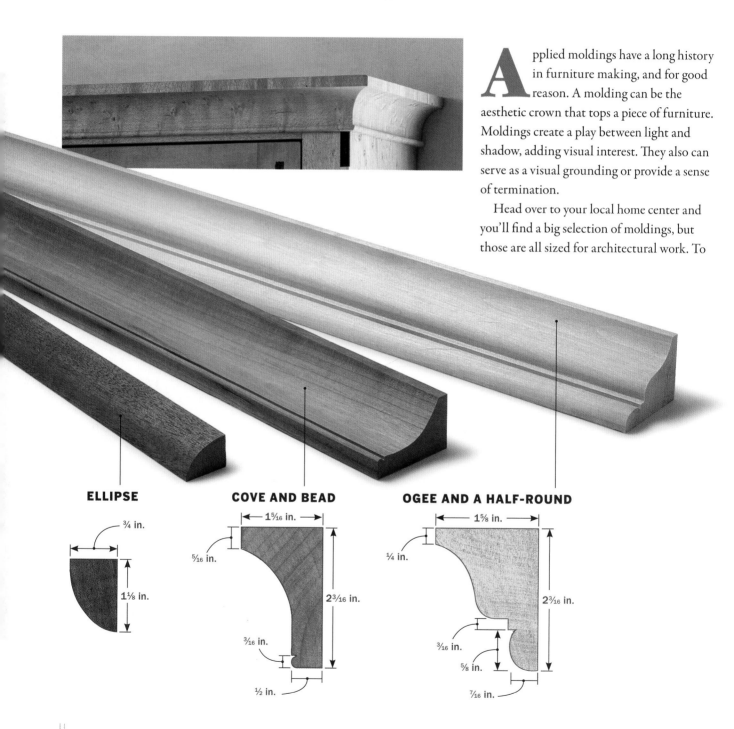

Applied moldings have a long history in furniture making, and for good reason. A molding can be the aesthetic crown that tops a piece of furniture. Moldings create a play between light and shadow, adding visual interest. They also can serve as a visual grounding or provide a sense of termination.

Head over to your local home center and you'll find a big selection of moldings, but those are all sized for architectural work. To

ELLIPSE

¾ in.

1⅛ in.

COVE AND BEAD

1⁵⁄₁₆ in.

⁵⁄₁₆ in.

2³⁄₁₆ in.

³⁄₁₆ in.

½ in.

OGEE AND A HALF-ROUND

1⅝ in.

¼ in.

2³⁄₁₆ in.

³⁄₁₆ in.

⅝ in.

⁷⁄₁₆ in.

get moldings proportioned for furniture, you need to make them. Perhaps the most common approach is to rout them, but then you're stuck using the profiles and proportions of the bits.

A better solution is to forgo the router altogether and create moldings with hand tools. It's not as hard as you might think. With a few planes, you can easily create graceful and beautiful custom profiles for your furniture that would be difficult or impossible with router bits. And there is no size limit, which allows you to dial in the proportions to complement the piece of furniture perfectly.

For a piece of furniture, you probably won't need more than several feet of molding. I've been making moldings this way for most of my career. Here, I'll show you how I do it.

Elegant ellipse with everyday tools. A block plane works great on convex curves. It's the only tool you need to transform the common quarter-round into a graceful quarter-ellipse.

Lay out the profile. Hack does this on the molding blank's leading edge, so he can gauge his progress as he removes waste at the tablesaw.

Power up. Angle the tablesaw blade to remove as much waste as possible in a single pass.

Plane away the facets. Start with thick shavings along the grain, and finish up with light shavings, which create smaller facets, resulting in a smoother curve.

Check the profile. To ensure consistency, Hack relies on a template made from a thin piece of wood.

Cove and bead are a refined pair. All it takes is a scratch stock to give the common cove a bit of panache. Size the bead to complement the cove's proportions.

Use hand tools where it counts

The majority (if not all) of the moldings you'll make will require you to remove a fair amount of waste material before you get to the task of shaping the profile. You could do that by hand, with a shoulder or rabbet

More cuts remove more waste. Speed up the work by taking several cuts with a tablesaw. To keep the molding stable throughout the process, remove the large chunk of waste on the bottom last.

Refine the cove with a round plane. Match the plane's radius to the cove's as closely as you can. If the cove's radius changes across the profile, switch out planes accordingly.

Begin the bead with a block plane. Roughing out the outside edge this way greatly speeds up the process of cutting the bead. Hack works to a layout line to rough in the bead.

Complete it with a scratch stock. This is the most accurate way to form a small bead. The cove needs to end in a narrow flat, as wide as the cutter.

Clean up with a scraper. To remove any ridges or tracks left by the round plane, use a gooseneck (shown). Rotate and angle the scraper to match the cove's curve.

plane, but I don't recommend it. Instead, use your tablesaw. This will let you get to the important job—creating the graceful lines of the molding—much faster.

Begin with a blank wider than the molding (you'll cut the molding free after it's made). After the tablesaw has eaten the waste, it's time for the handplanes to turn the roughed-out shape into a beautiful molding. The easiest profiles to handle are fillets and convex curves. Fillets are really just rabbets, and you can clean them up with a rabbet or shoulder plane. The right tool for convex curves is a block plane. (I rarely use hollow planes. They're troublesome to sharpen and set up.) Use a coarse setting to quickly remove material and get close to the final profile. Then switch to a fine cut, which leaves a smaller facet, making it easier to get a smooth curve from a tool that cuts flat surfaces.

Beauty built from an ogee and a half-round. Step away from the standard ogee by varying the curve's radius and create greater depth by adding a half-round at the bottom.

Clean fillet. A rabbet plane removes machining marks left by the tablesaw blade and creates a crisp line where the fillet transitions to the ogee.

Prop up the molding. Resting the molding on a piece of scrap brings the cove section of the ogee closer to vertical, making it easier to plane.

Concave curves are no more difficult than convex ones, except that you need a specialty plane to create them efficiently. Ideally, you'd use a round plane with a radius that closely matches the molding's profile, but it doesn't have to be perfect. Get as close as you can and then use a gooseneck scraper to get the rest of the way. The trick with the scraper is to find the section that matches the profile most closely, and then rotate it on its vertical axis until the scraper's edge is a perfect match. Or, if you're up for it, file a scraper to match the molding.

Finally, hand-sand the molding to remove any facets or bumps that are left.

Back to the block plane. Fair the convex curve, and create a smooth transition into the concave section.

Make the half-round on a separate piece. This allows you to create the entire curve with a block plane, rather than needing a specialized plane or a very large scratch stock.

Glue on the half-round. Yellow glue and a few clamps are all you need. Hack glues the part together on a piece of plywood, making it easier to keep the two parts flat and properly aligned.

Prep Rough Lumber with Hand Tools

ANDREW HUNTER

Flattening and dimensioning boards by hand is the bedrock of hand-tool woodworking. Nothing can teach you more about wood than taking it from rough to ready with a handplane. You'll improve your skill at reading the grain and sharpen your eye for a true surface. Through repetition, you'll develop a sense of controlled strength that will benefit every aspect of your work. And once you've developed the ability to mill by hand, your projects will no longer be limited by the size of your jointer and planer.

If possible, be kind to yourself with the species of wood you choose for hand milling. Softer woods free of knots and irregular grain are best. Most of the time, I mill a board in two separate stages: rough and finish. In the rough-milling stage, I first cut the board to rough length and width. Then I flatten the board, bringing it to within $\frac{1}{16}$ in. of final thickness. I remove the bulk of material from both sides without worrying about making perfectly smooth surfaces. I do this because a board needs to be somewhat flat before it can be made perfectly flat—if it bends under the pressure of planning, the springback will leave the board out of true. The two-stage process also allows me to let the rough-milled stock rest for a day or so—and move, if it's going to—before I plane it to finished thickness and smoothness.

To begin rough milling, shave the edges of the concave side of the board until, when

Start with the saw. Cut the parts ¼ in. oversize in length and width. You'll trim them to final size after the flattening is complete.

flipped, it will lie flat. Don't worry if it doesn't contact in the middle; your aim is just to get it stable. Now start the rough milling with the convex side of the board.

Whether you use Japanese handplanes like me, or Western ones, I recommend

Prepare the Board

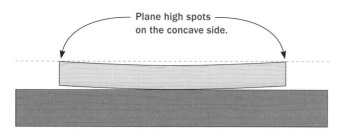

Plane high spots on the concave side.

Mark the highs and lows. Using a flat bench or table as a reference surface, find the high and low spots on both sides of the board and mark them with a pencil.

Take out the wobble. Working with a jack plane on the concave side of the board, plane flats along the two long edges until the board, when flipped, lies firmly without rocking.

TIP Knot-free wood is best for hand milling, but sometimes knots are unavoidable. To figure out which direction to plane over a knot, put a finger at the center of the knot on each side of the board. The offset between your fingers will indicate the angle of the knot. Plane with the angle. It also helps to soak a knot with water to soften it beforehand. The swollen cells will be less likely to tear out.

using three planes to do all the flattening: a scrub or jack plane (with its blade set for an aggressive cut), a jointer plane (long body for best jointing), and a smoother (short, wide body for a smooth final surface). The sequence of cuts with all the planes in the rough milling stage follows a similar pattern. Begin with strokes directly across the board—90° to the direction of the grain— and follow with strokes 60° to the grain, then

Start across the grain. Rough flattening starts with a short-bodied plane set to take a coarse shaving. Take strokes directly across the grain, skewing the plane slightly for a slicing cut.

Change Direction as You Go

In the rough-milling stage, plane in the sequence shown with the roughing, jointer, and smoothing planes. For the finish-milling stage, skip the roughing plane and omit angles 1 and 2.

45°, and finally along the grain. Take side-by-side strokes, overlapping them slightly. After you have rough-flattened the first face, set a marking gauge to ¹⁄₁₆ in. thicker than your intended final thickness and scribe a line around the board. Repeat the rough-milling process on the second side, working down to the scribe line. When you've finished, let the rough-milled board sit overnight (at least) with plenty of air circulation before final flattening.

Flatten One Face

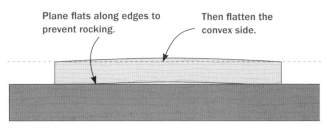

Plane flats along edges to prevent rocking.

Then flatten the convex side.

Check progress with a straightedge. Using a pencil, Hunter marks high spots with X's and squiggly lines, low spots with O's. Sighting across a pair of winding sticks will tell you if there's any twist in your planed surface.

Along the grain with a longer plane. After working through the angles with the roughing plane, follow up with a jointer plane. Use the same planning sequence of angled strokes, ending with passes along the grain. Then finish up with a smoothing plane, following the same sequence of strokes.

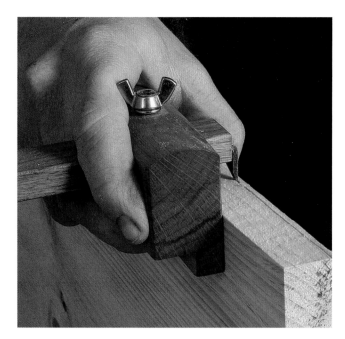

Leave it a little thick. Set a marking gauge to ¹⁄₁₆ in. over the board's final thickness. Working off the newly flattened surface, scribe a line around the workpiece.

Begin the finish milling with the show face. You can skip the roughing plane and start with your jointer plane. Also skip the 90° and 60° strokes. With the blade set for a fine shaving, take a series of strokes at 45° to the grain across the full width of the board and follow this with a sequence of strokes along the grain. Check with the straightedge and winding sticks, and if things look good, you're ready to clean up the surface with a freshly sharpened smoothing plane set very fine. Again, take strokes at 45° and then along the grain. Then use the marking gauge to scribe a line around the board to the final thickness, and finish-mill the second side, using the same sequence of strokes as on the show face and working right to the scribe line. Once the surfaces are flat, you can trim the board to final length and width.

Second side gets flattened. Repeat the same sequence of planes and planing angles to flatten the second side and bring the board to the marking gauge lines.

Shoot Edges on the Bench

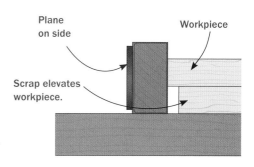

Plane on side

Workpiece

Scrap elevates workpiece.

Trim and square the edges.
By elevating the workpiece and using your plane on its side, you can use your bench like a shooting board and plane the board to final width (above left). After using a knife to lay out the finished length of the board and sawing just shy of the lines, use a jointer plane to trim to the scribe lines (left). To avoid blowing out the grain, take half passes with the plane, shaving from the outside toward the middle.

Don't Fear the Hand-Cut Dovetail

CHRISTIAN BECKSVOORT

I've been working wood for more than four decades now, and I've always considered hand-cut dovetails the bedrock of my furniture. Nothing else so clearly indicates strength, quality, and craftsmanship. Starting out, I tried making dovetails in a variety of ways—cutting the pins first, or the tails first; chopping out the waste between kerfs with a chisel, or sawing it away with a coping saw; using a Western saw or a Japanese one. Gradually, I developed a system that gave me strong, well-fitting, aesthetically pleasing joints at a very good clip. Over the years, I've continued to refine my method in subtle ways. Mine isn't the only approach to dovetails, but I think you'll find it straightforward, efficient, and relatively easy to master.

Pins vs. tails

The first book I consulted on dovetails recommended cutting the pins first. So did my father, a European-trained cabinetmaker. So I did. But I soon tried cutting the tails first, and I found it both faster and more accurate. Cutting tails first, you can clamp the two tail boards together and cut them at once. You not only save time sawing but you also increase accuracy, since the longer layout lines are easier to follow. I also think it's easier to trace the tails onto the pin board than the other way around, since the tail board can be laid flat while you trace it. Do pins first, and you have to hold the pin board

Layout. Becksvoort cuts both tail boards at once, so he needs to lay out the dovetail angles on only one of them.

Scribe the baseline. Adjust the marking gauge so its cutter just overhangs the pin board (above). The overhang will produce dovetails that are slightly proud. Scribe the baseline across both faces of the tail boards (right).

Anatomy of a Becksvoort Through-Dovetail

Becksvoort uses a standard chisel to lay out the pin sockets. His rule of thumb is to choose a chisel one size down from the thickness of the stock: for example, a ½-in.-wide chisel for ¾-in.-thick stock. He multiplies the chisel width by 2 to 2½ to get a rough idea for spacing between centerlines of the sockets.

Space the tails. To space out five tails evenly, Becksvoort angles a ruler from 0 in. to 10 in. and makes a mark every 2 in. That gives him the centerpoints of the four full-pin sockets.

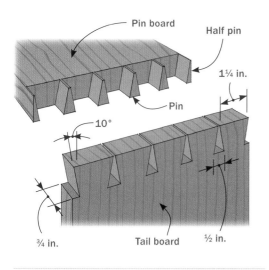

Transference. Use a square to transfer the center marks of the pin sockets to the end of the board.

vertically to mark the tail board. The transfer also is more precise when you do tails first, since it is done with a knife into end grain, the most accurate means of marking wood.

Mapping out tails and pins

The number and size of pins and tails has a huge bearing on the strength of a dovetail joint. The strongest possible joint would be 50% tails and 50% pins, but

that is aesthetically boring and resembles a machine-cut joint. Narrow pins are just more appealing. But don't take it too far. If you spread six ⅛-in.-wide pins across a 10-in.-wide board, you'll be removing almost 92% of the wood on the pin board and just 8% of the wood on the tail board. That sort of ratio may work on a delicate jewelry box or a small desk drawer, but on a cabinet or a large drawer, those joints will be far too

Mark them out. Establish the width of the pin sockets by tracing the chisel you'll use to chop them. Using a fine pencil, mark across the scribe line on each side of the chisel (left). Gauging by eye, make a mark for each of the half-pin sockets so they are roughly half the width of the full-pin sockets (right).

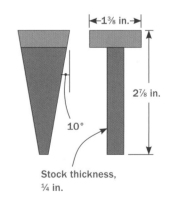

The essential angle. Using a dovetail gauge, mark from the baseline to the end of the board, angling from the side mark toward the centerline. Becksvoort made his gauge to match a Shaker chest he admired.

Saw the tails. Cut right to the layout lines. The tails are the template for the pins, so slight variations won't matter as long as the sawing is square.

Perfect posture. It's best to saw with your feet slightly apart and your forearm horizontal. With longer boards, if necessary, you can stand on a stable platform that raises you to a comfortable position.

Start the saw with a light touch. Begin cutting at the far side of the line, with the saw's handle elevated. As you saw, gradually drop the handle until the blade is engaged right across the board.

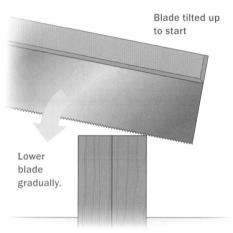

Blade tilted up to start

Lower blade gradually.

weak. As a compromise, I remove 70% to 80% of the wood on the pin board and 20% or 30% of the wood on the tail board. Don't get too hung up on the angle of the dovetails. There are passionate proponents for dovetail angles ranging anywhere from about 7° to 12°, but the practical difference is minimal. Outside that range, however, things get iffy. Angles above 15° result in weak corners on the tail board. And with angles below 5° or 6°, the dovetail begins to resemble a finger joint, losing its distinctive appearance and mechanical strength. I borrowed the angle of

TIP Pair up the tail boards. Clamp the two tail boards together in the vise with their sides and ends perfectly flush. Then carry the pin socket lines across the end grain of both boards. Cutting both boards at once improves accuracy, since the lines are longer and therefore easier to follow with the saw.

Cut one set, then the other. To maintain a good sawing rhythm—and maximum accuracy—first cut all the kerfs slanted in one direction, then go back and cut the ones slanted the other way.

TIP Oops. If your cut wanders far off track, start a new kerf parallel to the original pencil line. One of the tails will be slightly narrower than the others, but the angles will be consistent.

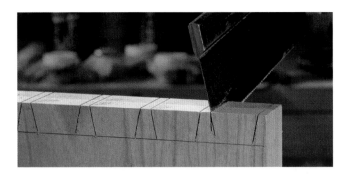

OFF TRACK? START ANEW

Make the new cut parallel to the original layout line.

Off-track kerf

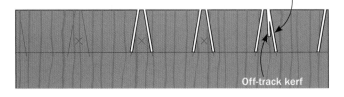

Reclamp and re-mark. To mark and cut the shoulders of the half-pin sockets, turn the tail boards 90° in the vise, being sure to keep all sides flush.

my dovetail marker, about 10°, from the first Shaker piece I restored, and I've been using it ever since.

Layout

Scribing the baselines with a marking gauge is the first step in the layout process. Any gauge with a sharp, knife-edge cutter will work. When I set the gauge, I let the cutter hang just over the edge of the board. This results in pins and tails that are slightly proud. Scribe both sides of both ends of all pieces.

Next, mark the centerpoints of the pin sockets. For efficiency, I make my pin sockets the width of a chisel (¼ in., ⅜ in., ½ in., ⅝ in., or ¾ in.). That way, they require only one setting of the chisel per socket. Use the chisel itself to lay out the sockets. Holding the chisel flat on the tail board with its blade crossing the scribed baseline and centered on the pin's centerline, draw marks on both sides of the blade. You can mark the width of the half sockets by eye. Then use a dovetail gauge and a pencil with a very fine point to draw the angled sides of all the sockets.

Last, bring the two tail boards together, inside face to inside face, exactly flush on the

Make it easy on yourself. Repositioning the boards is worth the trouble, since a vertical cut is much easier to make accurately.

sides and ends, and clamp them into a vise. Then use a square and a pencil to extend the layout lines across the end grain.

Sawing tails

Sawing to the line is usually the hardest part for most beginners. I recommend practicing on scrapwood until you learn the nuances of your saw and get a feel for its action. Stand comfortably, feet slightly apart, facing the boards. Optimally, your forearm should be horizontal.

Start the cut with the sawblade resting at the back of the square line and the handle slightly elevated. A light touch is required to start the cut. Just keep the saw moving,

Chop out the waste. Becksvoort takes a quick route to a flawless shoulder. Instead of trying to make a perfect shoulder the whole thickness of the workpiece, he makes a shallow shoulder right on the scribe line and then undercuts it.

Go lightly at first . . . Start straight up. Using the same chisel you used to lay out the pin sockets, seat the tip of the blade in the scribe line, hold the chisel perfectly vertical, and give it one light mallet hit. This creates a 90° shoulder right at the scribe line.

Pop out a slim chip. After lightly chopping all the pin sockets, use a narrower chisel to remove the top layer of waste wood with a tap into the end grain. The shoulder should now be about ¹⁄₁₆ in. high.

with no downward pressure. Then, as you saw, drop the handle of the saw so that you are cutting a full kerf along the pencil line. Once the kerf is established, slight downward pressure can be applied. Hold the saw at the same angle as the dovetail line and saw down to the scribe line. I like to saw all the right-tilting angles and then go back and saw the left-tilting ones, so I can get into a rhythm and let muscle memory take over.

Before putting the saw away, cut out the waste in the half sockets. It is definitely worth the time to reposition the boards so they are horizontal in the vise, since a vertical cut is much easier to make.

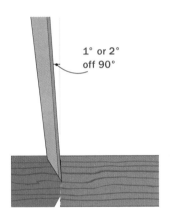

1° or 2° off 90°

Angle in for safety. Make the next series of chops using heavy mallet blows and holding the chisel so it angles toward you a degree or two. This undercuts the shoulder without changing it.

Then go heavy. Remove the thick waste chips and then resume chopping with the chisel angled. Continue chopping to the halfway point in the board's thickness.

Chopping between the tails

With both tail boards sawn, stack them on the bench, like stairs, and clamp. When making multiple drawers, I will stack up to six pieces at a time. This saves wear and tear on the arms. Constantly reclamping takes time and energy. If you clamp six pieces at once, for instance, you have to clamp only four

times. Clamp those same six boards individually, and you'll be clamping them 24 times!

Some folks like to stand, but working that way is hard on the back. I prefer to sit while chopping. The work should be at lower chest height, so your forearms are almost horizontal. A shop stool of the right height is essential.

Knife work. Use a sharp knife with a narrow blade to clean up the tight corners of the pin sockets.

I chop away the waste in two distinct steps: First I create a shallow, square shoulder on all the sockets; then I go back and remove the bulk of the waste with angled, undercutting strokes.

Begin by placing the layout chisel directly in the scribe line between the two sawcuts. Hold it at 90°, and give it one light tap with a mallet. Although the chisel is flat on the back, it is still a wedge, and too heavy a hit will widen the scribe line in both directions. Go up the stairs, making light hits on all the pin sockets. Then, with a narrower chisel, held horizontally with the bevel up, hit into the end grain to remove a chip of waste about 1/16 in. thick. This will leave you a nice, square shoulder directly on the scribe line.

Then comes stage two. Returning to the layout chisel, place its tip against the shoulder you've created. Tilt the handle toward you by a degree or two, and give it two hard hits with the mallet. This will undercut the joint slightly and ensure that the pins, when cut, will be tight against both inside and outside

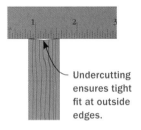

Undercutting ensures tight fit at outside edges.

Straightedge tells the tale. With the center of the shoulder undercut, a straightedge laid across the joint should contact only at the outside edges.

shoulders of the pin sockets. I use a chisel with very narrow flats on the sides to keep from deforming the tails.

Chop all the sockets this way, and then, with the smaller chisel, go along and remove a chip of waste about 1/8 in. thick from each one. Continue until you reach the center of the board. Then unclamp, flip, and restack the boards. Perform the same two-stage operation on the other side. As you approach the center of the joint, use light taps instead

Scribe the pins from the tails. Use a scrap block to support the tail board during scribing. First clamp the pin board in the vise so its top edge is flush with the block (left). Then move the block to support the far end of the tail board. If your boards are grooved for a bottom or back, insert a small square of wood into the groove to control side-to-side alignment (above).

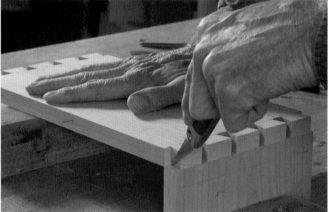

Knife work. Align the tail board so the gap between its shoulder and the face of the pin board is just barely closed (left). This will leave the ends of the tails proud by about the thickness of a fingernail. Trace the tails onto the end grain of the pin board (right), starting with a light stroke and following with one or two heavier ones.

of heavy ones until the waste pops down and forward. If you're not careful, you can ruin the shoulder on the other side and hit the workpiece below.

Since the sawcuts are at about 80° and the edge of the chisel is at 90°, there is usually a small bit of waste wood left in the corners of

the pin sockets that needs to be removed. Use a sharp, narrow knife to clean these corners. Finally, place a chisel or a square across the inside of the sockets and sight across it to be sure that the joint is properly undercut—low in the middle and with the shoulders as the high points.

At this stage, if you've sawn square across and straight down to the scribe lines, and chopped correctly, you're still on track for a perfect dovetail. The tail boards you've produced are the templates for the next step.

Transfer the tails with precision

When you're making hand-cut dovetails, transferring the first half of the joint to the second half is where the rubber hits the road. Accurate scribing is essential. Luckily, two of the big benefits to cutting tails first and pins second come into play as you make the transfer. One is that you can lay the tail board flat as you trace the tails. The other is that you can make the marks with a knife into end grain for maximum accuracy. Before you begin tracing the tails, number the mating joints—1,1; 2,2; 3,3; 4,4—so it's clear which sets of pins belong with which sets of tails.

I use a simple trick to keep the tail board flat and steady while I scribe. Place a square block on the benchtop in front of the vise. Then clamp the pin board in the vise so its top end is flush with the top face of the block. Now when you set one end of the tail board on the pin board for scribing, you can use the scrap to support the other end.

Align the tail board so that its sides are flush with the sides of the pin board. Then line up the shoulders of the tails with the inside face of the pin board. The tails, which will be proud in the finished joint, will protrude slightly past the outside face of the pin board.

Holding the tail board down firmly with one hand, mark along both cheeks of all the tails. Use a sharp knife with a long bevel and hold the bevel flat against the wood. For maximum accuracy, make a light cut first, followed by a heavier cut. Then use a square and a fine-point pencil to carry these knifed

Finish the layout. Use a square and a pencil with a fine point to draw the lines between the scribed angles and the scribed baseline.

Saw and chop the waste. Your kerf should be right on the knife and pencil lines. Mark the waste with Xs to avoid mistakes.

Strike lightly. With the chisel held upright and its point in the scribed baseline, establish the shoulder with a light mallet blow.

First chip is the slimmest. Remove a thin chip of waste with a tap on a horizontal chisel, and you'll have a 1/16-in.-deep square shoulder. To chop out the rest of the waste, hold the chisel just off vertical—tilted toward you—and use harder mallet blows. This undercuts the joint, leaving the shoulder intact.

lines down the faces of the pin board to the baseline.

Remove the waste between pins

When you cut the pins, your sawkerfs should, ideally, be right on the layout lines. You could saw close to the lines and pare to them later, but this is a slow and inefficient process. Better to put the extra time into practicing cutting to a line beforehand.

Once all the pins are sawn, you can move on to chopping out the waste. Clamp the pin boards flat on the bench, stacked like steps, and begin by establishing the shoulder. Use a wide chisel held vertically and with its point right in the scribed baseline. Make one light mallet blow at each setting of the chisel—you'll likely have to set the chisel twice to span the baseline from pin to pin—and chop between all the pins. This light chop establishes the shoulder without driving the chisel beneath the baseline.

Use the same wide chisel held horizontally to tap into the end grain and take out a chip of waste about 1/16 in. thick. Now you have

Same sequence on side two. After chopping to the middle of the pin boards, flip them and use the same techniques to establish a square shoulder and chop away the waste on the other side. Lighten up at the end to avoid damaging the shoulder below.

Pare for a perfect fit. If any of your scribed lines are visible on the end grain, put the tip of a chisel in the line and pare away the waste (left). If the grain is running into the pin, pare from the side instead of the top (right).

a shallow, square shoulder. The rest of the joint will be undercut slightly, speeding up the process and leaving the shallow shoulder pristine. You can afford to undercut, since this is all end grain and is not a good glue surface anyway.

With the chisel tilted toward you slightly, make each chop with several firm mallet blows. Chop between all the pins and follow up by removing a thick chip of waste.

Continue chopping this way between all the pins until you reach the middle of the boards. Then flip them, reclamp, and repeat the two-step chiseling process from the other face. When you are working on the last bit of waste, use a series of light hits to avoid damaging the shoulder and stock below.

With the chopping finished, clamp each pin board in the vise in turn and examine the end grain. If any of the scribe lines are visible,

Gauge the fit with graphite. Blacken the first ⅛ in. or so of the tails' cheeks with a pencil (left). Engage the joint evenly with moderate fist pressure (center). Where the graphite has transferred to the pins, pare it away gingerly, coming from the top if the grain permits (right), or from the side if the grain is tricky.

Knock it home. After paring the pencil marks away, test the fit again, disengaging the boards and reapplying graphite as often as necessary until the joint slides snugly home.

Low-stress glue-up. To simplify the glue-up, assemble the box so the joints are just barely engaged. Then apply glue to the cheeks of all the pins and tails before pounding the joints home.

you have paring to do. Select a chisel that's wider than the pin, put its point in the scribe line, and pare straight down. Be careful of the grain here; if it runs in toward the pin and pulls the chisel with it, try paring from the side instead of from the top. After paring, use a knife to clean out all the inside corners. Finally, check with a square to see that the joints are properly undercut—the shallow shoulders you established on each face of the board should be the high points.

Pare the pins to fit the joint

In a perfect world, you would now be able to drive the joints all the way home with moderate fist blows. But in reality, fitting comes next. Always do this paring and fitting on the pins; the tail board is the pattern, and the pins must conform to it.

With a pin board in the vise, align the matching tail board and press down lightly. If the two pieces barely engage, that's good. Remove the tail board and, with a pencil, darken the leading edges of the tails. Re-engage the pieces and pound a bit harder.

Use clamps if you need them. After pounding the joints home, use clamps if necessary to close any gaps and to adjust the box for squareness.

Easy squeeze. Becksvoort doesn't need specially made clamping blocks to contend with the proud tails. He just makes white pine blocks, which are soft enough to conform to the proud parts of the joint.

Where the graphite has transferred onto the pins, pare ever so slightly, keeping the chisel vertical. Don't undercut, since this is your glue surface. If the joint is already engaging, don't pare all the way from the top of the pin, since it already fits there. Be patient; it may take three, four, or even five tries before you get a good fit.

If there are gaps between any of the pins and tails, you'll need remedial action after the glue-up (see pp. 172–173).

Tricks for a confident glue-up

For small glue-ups, you can coat the pins and tails with glue while the parts are separate and assemble as normal. But for medium and large glue-ups, partially engage all four corners—by ⅛ in. or so—before applying any glue. Then use a narrow stick to apply glue to the exposed faces of the tails and pins on all four corners. Pound the joints together with a caul and mallet. If the joints don't come completely home with the mallet, use clamps. I use scraps of pine as clamping pads. Even though the joints are proud, there's no need for custom clamping blocks. The pine conforms easily to the shape of the joint while delivering the clamping pressure. If there's much glue squeeze-out, slip a piece of waxed paper under the pine to keep the blocks from adhering to the workpiece.

A Fine Fix for Gaps

As the glue dries, examine the joints. If there are any hairline gaps between the pins and tails, you can fill them with commercial wood filler or with a homemade recipe: ⅔ glue to ⅓ water, to the consistency of heavy cream, then blend in sanding dust (not sawdust) to the consistency of peanut butter. With white or yellow glue, avoid contacting metal while you mix and apply the filler, since the glue will react with the metal and turn black.

Larger gaps—the width of a sawkerf or less—can be fixed after the clamps are off. Widen the gap with a handsaw. Then cut a thin shim from a scrap that matches your project and glue it into the kerf. Depending on which direction you insert it from, the shim's grain will match either the pin or the tail.

Create a kerf-size shim. Using the tablesaw and a scrap of stock that matches your project, cut a shim that fits your handsaw's kerf.

Kerf the corner. To repair a gap between a pin and a tail, start by sawing into the gap with the blade on a 45° angle. Cut the kerf from baseline to baseline.

Trim the shim. Cut one end of the shim on a 45° angle with the chop of a chisel. After gluing it in place, trim the shim flush (right) with a few strokes of a knife.

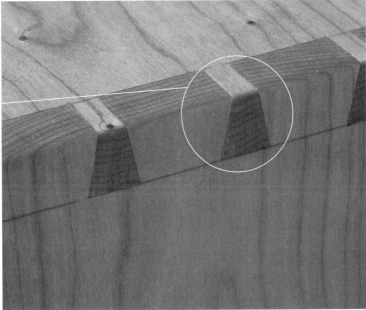

Seamless repair. Glued in with its side grain and end grain matching the neighboring pin (above), this shim is virtually invisible once it's sanded flush (right).

PART THREE

PROJECTS

Build Your Own Handsaw

TOM CALISTO

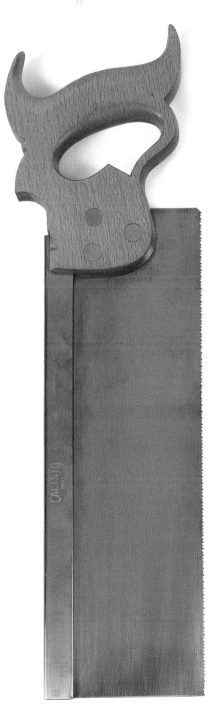

Handsaws are a great introduction to tool making. The parts are few and readily available, and there's no huge investment in time or money to create a top-notch saw that fits your hand perfectly. The only tasks that require care are shaping the handle and cutting the slot for the blade and the mortise for the spine, both of which are easy for a furniture maker to tackle.

Whether you make a dovetail saw or carcase saw, the process is the same. Here I'll illustrate the project using a closed-handled carcase saw (near right), but I have included a design for a dovetail saw (far right). The carcase saw is my adaptation of an old Disston® pattern. The 3-in.-wide by 12-in.-long blade is a great size for cutting joinery—tenons, notches, or miters—and cutting parts to final length. I tweaked the handle design and some dimensions to end up with a classic-style saw that fits the hand better than the original.

Rough out the handle

I chose European beech for the handle because it's fairly hard, closed-grained, and not prone to splitting. Cherry and walnut are also great choices.

Start by tracing the pattern onto ⅞-in.-thick stock, aligning the grain so that it runs in line with the saw plate. Make the exterior cuts at the bandsaw and the interior on the scrollsaw. After the pattern has been cut out, remove the milling marks with a rasp, but don't start shaping yet.

Two Handle Angles

A saw's hang refers to the angle of the grip in relation to the tooth line. It plays a critical role in the way the saw handles.

CARCASE SAW

A carcase saw has a low handle angle that directs most of the cutting force forward along the tooth line and relies on the saw's weight to apply pressure.

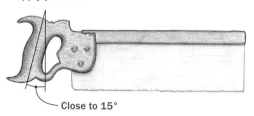

Close to 15°

DOVETAIL SAW

A dovetail saw has a more severe handle angle, which helps the lighter-weight saw direct more pressure downward and into the cut.

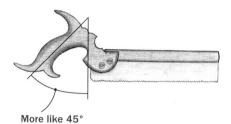

More like 45°

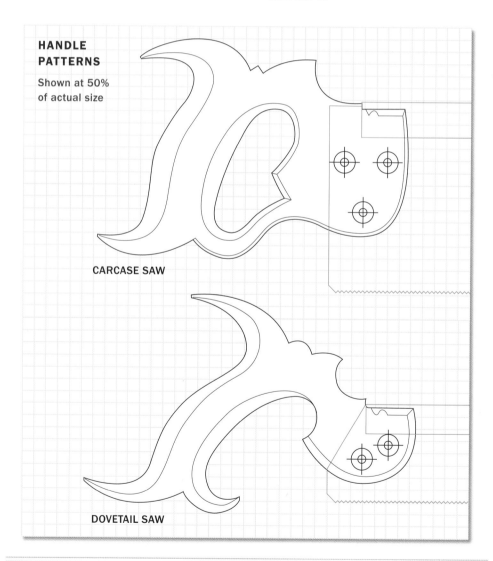

HANDLE PATTERNS

Shown at 50% of actual size

CARCASE SAW

DOVETAIL SAW

Cut the handle to size. After laying out the handle's shape on the blank, saw out the exterior at the bandsaw and the interior at the scrollsaw (above). Fair the edges (right), using a rasp to clean up the millmarks left by the bandsaw. Be sure to keep the faces perpendicular to the sides.

Cut the slot for the saw plate

Sawing an accurate slot is a critical step, and I always saw the slot for the plate and mortise for the spine before doing any shaping. This way, you can use the flat and parallel sides to mark for the joinery.

Start by establishing the plate's depth in the handle. Assemble the plate and spine and place the assembly on the handle with the spine parallel to the flat on the nose of the handle blank and roughly ⅛ in. above it. Mark the depth of the plate along the sides and the top and bottom edges of the handle. It is important to have enough room for the saw nuts to engage the plate without having them right on the edge of the handle.

After marking the depth of cut, set up a marking gauge to scribe a line marking the slot for the saw plate. Scribe all the way along the edge of the handle between the layout marks.

Make way for the saw plate and spine. To start, lay out the slot depth. Set the plate on the handle and mark both sides of the handle where the slot will end. Transfer these marks across the edges as well.

The quickest way to cut the slot is to use another backsaw with a similar kerf. If you're a little shaky with a saw or this will be your first saw, I have a simple trick to make this task painless.

First, you'll need the toothed and sharpened saw plate and some hardwood

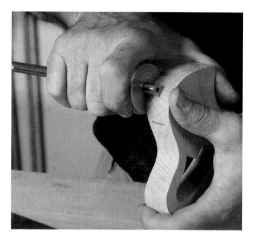

Mark a cut line. Set a marking gauge to half the thickness of the handle and score a line between the two edge marks.

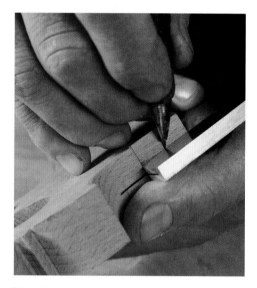

Mark for the spine mortise. Put the spine on the plate, slide it all the way to the back of the slot, and lower it onto the top of the handle. Mark the mortise length. Then mark the depth of the mortise by placing the spine on the front edge of the handle.

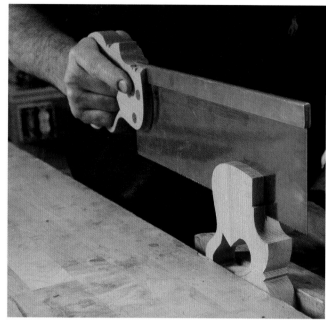

Saw the slot. Clamp the handle upright and saw the slot into the handle following the marking-gauge line. It's vital that this slot is straight and doesn't waver.

TIP Error-proof slotting option. If you don't own a saw yet or aren't confident in your sawing skills, clamp the blade to the bench between two pieces of hardwood. The bottom piece must be milled to half the thickness of the handle, which will place the slot exactly where it needs to be. Draw the handle against the blade until the slot is cut.

scraps. Mill a piece of scrap to half the thickness of the handle material; this will space the plate off the bench to cut a perfectly centered slot. Lay the saw plate on top of the spacer, put another piece of scrap over it, and clamp it to the bench with the teeth pointing away from you. Lay the handle flat on the bench and draw it back over the saw plate until the slot reaches the depth marks. When

you're done, you should have a perfectly straight slot for the saw plate.

Mortise for the spine

To mortise the handle for the spine, insert the spine and saw plate as a single assembly into the slot with the back of the plate flat against the slot in the handle and the spine against the top edge of the handle. Pencil around the spine to mark the mortise length (see the bottom left photo on the facing page). Then reposition the assembly so that the spine is against the front of the handle to define the depth, and remember to leave the back about ⅛ in. proud of the handle.

Carefully chisel out the mortise. Check the fit to make sure the entire assembly sits straight in the slot and mortise. Once it's perfect, you can move on to shaping the handle.

Handwork for the handle

Getting the handle symmetrical and comfortable can seem daunting, but with careful layout it's simple. Begin by drawing a centerline down the handle and adding some chamfer lines along the edges. The chamfer lines are guides for removing the bulk of the

Shape the handle. Use pencil lines to guide the work. Mark a centerline along the entire outside edge of the handle and mark chamfer lines in the grip area so that you can evenly remove the bulk of the material for shaping.

Rasp removes the waste quickly. Start with a rasp and work down to the chamfer lines. Work with the grain to avoid tearout.

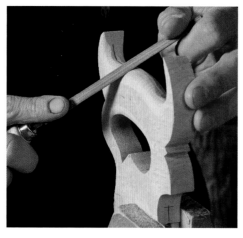

Ease the transitions. Use the rasp to ease the chamfers into complete curves. Be sure to check the grip with your hand to make sure the shape is a good fit.

Round the hard edges. The horns at the top and bottom of the grip are rounded off with a rasp. The remaining interior profiles and lower edges of the handle's exterior can be lightly pillowed.

Drill the handle. Start with pilot holes. After marking the locations of the saw nuts, drill a $\frac{1}{16}$-in. pilot hole for each one. This will ensure the multiple holes and bores are aligned from side to side.

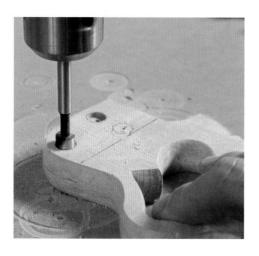

Saw-Nut Holes Must Align Perfectly

Each saw-nut hole has counterbores for the heads on each end, a standard hole for the shank, and a square mortise for the square shoulder.

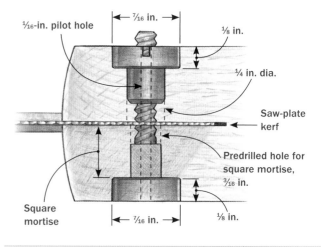

$\frac{1}{16}$-in. pilot hole

$\frac{7}{16}$ in.

$\frac{1}{8}$ in.

$\frac{1}{4}$ in. dia.

Saw-plate kerf

Predrilled hole for square mortise, $\frac{3}{16}$ in.

Square mortise

$\frac{7}{16}$ in.

$\frac{1}{8}$ in.

Counterbore for the heads. Use a Forstner bit in the drill press to counterbore for the head of the saw nuts on both sides of the handle. Set the depth stop to leave the saw nuts just proud of the handle. The nuts will be leveled flush later.

Drill for the shank and shoulder. The shoulder of the saw nut is square and one side of the handle needs to be bored—and later chiseled—to match. Drill the bore for the square shoulder and stop at the saw plate slot. Flip the handle and drill for the shank of the saw nut.

Square up the hole. Chisel the round hole square to match the shoulder on the saw nuts. The fit doesn't have to be perfect, but it must be snug to keep the nut from spinning.

material equally. Start the shaping process with the grip area. Rasp off the corners to the chamfer lines and round over this section with a file and sandpaper. The shape should be elliptical in the grip area, flow nicely into the other sections of the handle, and most important, feel good in your hand.

The sharp-edged horns on the back of the handle also get rounded, and the underside of the handles and other inside faces of the grip cutout can be pillowed with a soft roundover. After roughing things out with rasps, move on to files and finally sandpaper.

Drill the handle and plate for the saw nuts

The brass fasteners that hold the saw plate to the handle are called saw nuts. To make these fit and function, the handle must be bored for the shoulders, heads, and shanks of the nuts. All these bores need to align on both sides of the handle, so start at the drill press, drilling a 1/16-in. pilot hole through the handle at each saw-nut location. The pilot hole will guide subsequent bits from either side of the handle. Drill the counterbores for the saw-nut heads with a Forstner bit, leaving the holes slightly shallow so the head will be slightly proud of the handle. Next, drill one side for the screw shank and square it with a chisel to accept the screw's square shoulder. Drill the opposite side slightly larger to accept the shoulder of the nut.

There are several ways to make the holes in the saw plate, but the best I've found is a straight-fluted carbide drill bit in the drill press. Just make sure that the teeth are going in the right direction before you drill. I have seen a few push saws morph into pull saws.

Drill the saw plate. With the spine attached to the plate and seated full in the slot, mark one of the saw-nut locations with a transfer punch.

Drill the first hole. For the greatest accuracy, use a straight-fluted carbide bit in the drill press to make the first hole. Clamping the thin blade to the table and against a fence is a must.

Reinstall the saw plate. Clean up the burrs from the drill press and install the plate with one saw nut. Then transfer the locations of the remaining two holes to the saw plate and drill those as well.

Assemble all the components, line everything up, then mark one hole with a transfer punch. It's important to start with only one hole first to prevent misalignment. Pull the saw apart and drill the first hole. Drilling thin sheet stock can be dangerous, so make sure everything is clamped down; otherwise, you risk having a saw plate swinging around at 1,000 rpm.

Once the first hole is drilled, remove any burrs with a file and reassemble the saw. Place a saw nut into the first hole, mark the others, and drill those in the same way. If the holes don't line up perfectly, adjust them by opening the holes slightly with a round file.

Pinching the spine. A few good smacks with a dead-blow mallet will tighten up the spine. Calisto uses a log as an anvil, but a sturdy bench works too.

Round over the spine. A shopmade scraper rounds the spine to look like a traditional folded spine. The same effect can be done with files and sandpaper.

Soften the end. A file quickly and effectively gives the end of the spine a slightly rounded profile.

Pinch the spine

The spine is the last major component and is attached to the plate with a friction fit, which means the slot in the spine is squeezed to clamp the saw plate in place. The spine comes fitted loosely to the plate. While building a saw, I take the spine on and off many times, so I find it easier to pinch them together as a final step.

The most effective way to pinch the spine is to use a dead-blow hammer to close the gap. Angle the hammer and concentrate the blows on the slotted side, taking the time to sneak up on the fit. It should be tight enough that a few light mallet blows will seat the

A quick polish. Whether it's a uniform sanding with 320-grit sandpaper or a full polishing, clean up the spine to get it ready for installation on the plate.

plate on the back, but not so tight that it is impossible to start.

As a final touch, I use a small, shopmade scraper to round over the spine and give it a more traditional look. Once you've shaped the whole top of the spine, smooth the

Slowly seat the back. After installing the plate in the handle, line up the spine with the mortise and tap on the spine gradually until it is seated fully on the plate.

roundover and either sand the spine to a uniform luster with 320-grit paper, or polish it fully.

Put it all together

Final assembly begins with joining the saw plate to the handle. Slide the plate into the handle and insert the saw nuts. Don't force the saw nuts into the handle; the steel plate can easily strip the brass threads. Lightly tighten the saw nuts, as the spine must be installed before fully torquing the fasteners.

Align the spine flush with the back wall of the mortise and place the sawteeth on a soft wood block. Gently tap the spine with a soft mallet or dead-blow mallet to drive it onto the plate. Work your way along the spine, driving it deeper with each pass. Do this gradually to avoid bending or twisting the saw plate.

File down the saw nuts. Take down the threaded portion and head on each saw nut until it's just shy of flush.

With the spine seated, tighten the fasteners and flush the saw nuts to the handle—first with a file, then with sandpaper on a flat surface. Last, give the handle a final sanding and polish the metal parts with fine steel wool. I finish the handle with wipe-on polyurethane, a durable and easy-to-apply finish. I apply it to the assembled saw and use mineral spirits to clean up anything that gets on the saw plate or spine. After three coats, lightly rub out the surface with a nonwoven abrasive pad and apply some paste wax to the entire saw.

Sources of Supply

BLACKBURN TOOLS
www.blackburntools.com

TWO GUYS IN A GARAGE TOOLWORKS
www.tgiag.com

CALISTO TOOLS
www.windwardwoodworks
.com

Lap the sides flat. Sandpaper glued to a sheet of Baltic-birch plywood is flat enough to level the brass saw nuts and handle sides to a uniform plane.

Finish when fully assembled. Calisto uses wipe-on polyurethane to finish saw handles because it is durable and easy to use. Use mineral spirits to clean off any finish that lands on the saw plate.

Wax the whole thing. When the finish is dry, a layer of wax over the entire saw will protect the handle, blade, and spine from dirt and moisture.

Custom Scrapers for Custom Work

GARRETT HACK

Few tools are as simple as a card scraper, or as versatile and effective. It's just a rectangle of flexible steel with a fine burr for a cutting edge, but it can perfectly smooth the most ornery grain. I take that basic idea a bit further, making custom scrapers of all kinds. Typically these small tools, for working in tight places, have curved or angled edges, and most of the time no burr at all.

Better than sandpaper

What makes a scraper so useful is its ability to cut a very fine shaving in any direction, against or with the grain, around curves as well as on flat parts, and to cut well at any angle to the surface. Scrapers can level flat surfaces and fair shaped ones. And a well-sharpened scraper cuts more quickly and cleanly than sandpaper, with more control.

My collection of custom scrapers can be divided into two categories: those with

Cut and shape the steel. Hack cuts small scrapers from an old Japanese handsaw blade (left). More robust scrapers are taken from thicker Western saws. For a straight scraper, he snips it out of the blank, then cleans up the cuts with a file (above), holding the blank in a small vise.

Hone and polish. Hack hones the edges of the scraper on a fine diamond plate and a 2,000-grit waterstone. He polishes the faces first on the 2,000-grit waterstone and finishes with 5,000 grit. He polishes only the area near the cutting edge. For these cleanup tools, a burr is not necessary.

straight edges and those with curved edges. Straight edges generally work best on flat areas, such as when scraping squeeze-out from a joint or lightly leveling a surface after applying finish. Some of my straight scrapers have corners where the edges meet

just shy of 90° to allow me to reach into tight corners easily.

My curved-edge scrapers can smooth any concave or convex surface, stepping in after a router or molding plane does its work. My most basic scrapers have simple round shapes for such tasks as fine-tuning a mitered corner

Adding curves. After cutting the blank to size, use a fine Sharpie to trace the profile on it (left). Shape the profile with a file, then hone the edge and polish the faces in the same way you'd work a square-edge scraper (right). For hollows, you'll need a chainsaw file or jeweler's files to create the profile. Don't use a grinder with this thin steel, as it will ruin the temper.

Perfect a profile without losing detail. This curly maple molding had some tearout. To clean it up without losing detail, Hack uses a rounded scraper for the concave section (left), and a square scraper to finish the fillet (above).

in a cove molding. A few have a combination of shapes that fit a whole molding profile. They take longer to make, but they are especially useful for fairing and smoothing curved moldings. Oftentimes, though, I'll use a handful of different shaped scrapers on complex moldings instead of trying to file multiple shapes onto one tool.

Simple to make

The steel I use to make my scrapers is the same spring-tempered steel of a card scraper. I use old handsaws for thicker, stiffer scrapers, and worn-out Japanese saws for thin and flexible ones. This steel is soft enough that it can be filed, yet hard enough to hold an edge. Strong snips work to cut the scraper to rough shape, and files are used to get a final profile. Stay away from a grinder or you risk burning the thin steel and ruining its temper.

For the small shaped scrapers, I draw the profile I want on the blank with a Sharpie® and file the steel to that line. If you are creating a scraper with a concave profile, you'll need some round files of different diameters. If you want a scraper to match a molding profile or part of it, trace the molding on the steel blank. As you file, make sure you maintain a square edge. When you're done, it should feel sharp even before you start to hone.

After filing the scrapers, I hone their edges using a fine diamond plate and a 2,000-grit waterstone. The most important part of the process is to keep the blank perfectly perpendicular as you hone, to ensure a square edge. At this point the tool already feels sharp and is able to make some shavings. I hone the faces of the scraper next, focusing near the cutting edge only. For this I use 2,000-grit and 5,000-grit waterstones.

I don't put a burr on these scrapers. They work very well without one. The scraper should produce delicate shavings, no matter whether you push or pull it across the surface. The only time I put a burr on my custom scrapers is if I need to take a more aggressive cut, say, if my goal is to alter the shape of a profile. A scraper's cutting edge never lasts that long, but honing it again to sharpen it is very quick.

Custom scrapers are a real asset to your tool collection. Try one, and before long you'll be making more of them and using sandpaper far less.

Clean up the cock bead. For this delicate job, Hack uses the straight-edge scraper to get the glue out. Again, the vertical edge of the scraper has a slight angle so it can reach into the corner without damaging the applied bead.

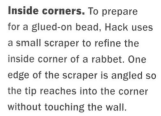

Inside corners. To prepare for a glued-on bead, Hack uses a small scraper to refine the inside corner of a rabbet. One edge of the scraper is angled so the tip reaches into the corner without touching the wall.

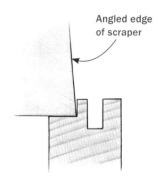

Angled edge of scraper

Beadwork. This ebony bead is smoothed with a narrow scraper with a hollow nose that matches the bead profile. A light touch creates delicate shavings.

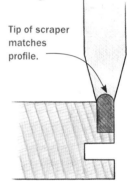

Tip of scraper matches profile.

Leg-to-apron joint. Squeeze-out on an inset apron is hard to reach, but a small, thin scraper is the solution. You can run it across the grain without damage (left), or scrape out the glue from the corner with the grain (right).

They work for finishes, too. Hack uses wider square-edge scrapers to remove dust nibs and other imperfections from tabletop finishes. A well-honed scraper will leave a glasslike surface.

Make a Pair of Grooving Planes

MATTHEW KENNEY

When I make a cabinet with small drawers or a box with trays, I enjoy the time at my workbench making and fitting the parts with hand tools and a few bench jigs. Unfortunately, the efficiency and tranquility of my work were always interrupted when it came time to make grooves for the bottom panels, a task I did at the router table or tablesaw.

One day it hit me: The grooves I use for small tray and drawer bottoms are always the same size and are inset the same distance from the edge, so I don't need a power tool that can cut grooves of various widths or has an adjustable fence. A molding plane that cuts a groove rather than a profile would be a simple solution. So I made a pair of grooving planes with integral fences. A pair is needed so that you can always cut with the grain. They plow a perfect groove in about a minute, with no setup needed. By the way, you can make your set larger if you wish, and use it for full-size drawers.

Body is a three-part sandwich

I like using planes, not making them, so I made these using a simple technique

191

Start with the Blades

This plane is built around the blade, so get that first. You can make your own from tool steel, as I used to do. But after I showed my planes to Thomas Lie-Nielsen, he offered to make and sell the blades. A pair costs $50 (www.lie-nielsen.com). Lie-Nielsen sells similar blanks in other sizes. You'll just need to bevel and heat-treat these yourself.

popularized by James Krenov. A middle piece, cut in two to form the bed, throat and mouth, is laminated between two sides. (On this plane, the middle piece also acts as the skate, controlling the depth of the groove.)

Because you cut apart the middle piece at the tablesaw, it is easy to get a perfectly formed bed, throat, and mouth. Mortising and filing are not needed.

I use beech for the sides, but you could use any hard, stable wood. I start with a 5/4 board about 18 in. long because I make two planes at once and it is safer milling a longer board. Resaw the board into two pieces, just over ½ in. and ⅜ in. thick. After jointing the resawn faces, plane the boards to final thickness. I rip the thicker, wider board to width, rout a rabbet on the side that will have the fence, and then rip the other side to width. At this point, I crosscut both pieces twice. This breaks apart the two long pieces, leaving me with the four sides of two planes.

Now joint and plane a core piece from any hard, durable wood, so its thickness is equal to the blade's width. At the tablesaw, crosscut the stock to form the bed and throat pieces.

Fit the wedge and add finishing touches

Start by gluing the bed and throat pieces to the side with the fence. Line up the top, back,

Shopmade Grooving Plane

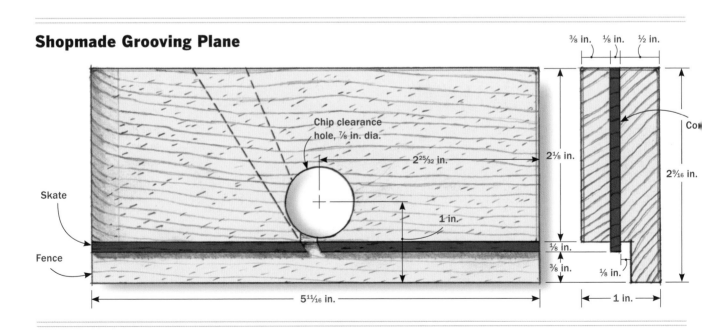

Chip clearance hole, ⅞ in. dia.

2²⁵⁄₃₂ in.

2⅛ in.

1 in.

Skate

Fence

5¹¹⁄₁₆ in.

⅜ in. ⅛ in. ½ in.

2⁹⁄₁₆ in.

⅛ in.

⅜ in. ⅛ in.

1 in.

Start with the Sides

Side, ⅜ in. thick by 2⅛ in. tall

Fence side, ½ in. thick by 2⁹⁄₁₆ in. tall

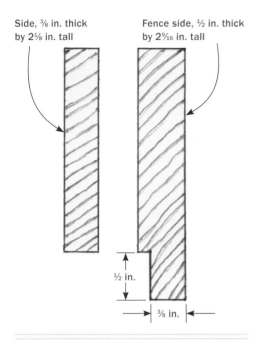

½ in.

⅜ in.

Rabbet one side. Once you rip the piece to width, use a router table to create the rabbet that will act as the fence.

Rip the other side to fit. Kenney lines up the tablesaw fence with the top of the rabbet to get the exact width of the narrower side, and then rips that side to size.

Add the Core

Cut the core into two parts. Square up one end of the core and then set the miter gauge to the bed angle. Cut the bed to length. Cut the throat angle and then crosscut the throat piece to size.

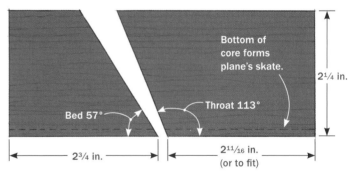

Bottom of core forms plane's skate.

2¼ in.

Bed 57°

Throat 113°

2¾ in.

2¹¹⁄₁₆ in. (or to fit)

Glue the bed to the fence side. Before tightening down the clamp, let the glue tack up slightly and feel around the edges for the precise alignment.

Set the blade in place to mark the throat opening. Leave enough clearance for the blade to fit through, plus about ¹⁄₆₄ in. for chip clearance.

Pencil line and outside edges guide placement. Glue the throat piece in place, eyeballing it and feeling for alignment.

Make the Wedge

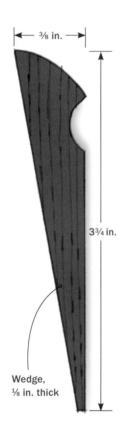

3/8 in.

3 3/4 in.

Wedge, 1/8 in. thick

Fit the wedge in the partially assembled plane. Test-fit the wedge. If the angle isn't quite right, mark the wedge and tweak the angle to fit using sandpaper on a flat surface. Test the fit and repeat as needed to get a tight fit along both the front of the throat and the blade.

and front edges with your fingers to ensure that the bed and throat are at the right angles. Clamp them in place, taking care that no glue ends up in the throat. Begin to make the wedge from the same piece of stock used to make the bed and throat pieces. Cut it oversize at the bandsaw and tweak the fit with sandpaper. After fitting the wedge, cut the top. You'll cut it to length (at the bottom) after you finish gluing the body together. Glue on the second side of the plane body.

After removing the clamps, drill the chip-clearance hole. It also makes a great finger hold, so chamfer its edges for comfort. I used a trim router and chamfer bit, but a file or sandpaper works. Next, round over the edges of the plane. Now, take a few light shavings off the skate on the side that doesn't face the fence so that it won't bind in the groove. Then cut back the bottom tip of the wedge so that shavings don't get jammed in the mouth. Cut it, plane a groove, and repeat until the plane is clearing shavings without trouble.

I finish the plane with two thin coats of Tried & True™ Danish oil, wiping off the excess after each.

Shape the top of the wedge. Mark the shape and cut it out on the bandsaw, and sand it to a finished smoothness. It should be about ½ in. below the top of the blade. Kenney adds a finger notch.

Add the second side. After the wedge is finished, glue on the second side, again waiting for the glue to tack slightly and aligning the pieces by feel before clamping.

Big hole helps clear shavings. Use a Forstner bit at the drill press to cut a hole that meets the bed but does not cut into it (left). To help the chips reach the hole, saw a slot that lines up with the mouth (above).

Round over sharp edges. On the back end of the plane, where your hand wraps around it, Kenney uses a ½-in.-dia. roundover bit in a router table. A backer board prevents tearout on the end grain and improves the plane's stability as you guide it past the bit. He breaks the rest of the sharp edges with sandpaper.

Using the plane

There is no learning curve here. Use a sharp blade, set for a slightly heavier cut than for a smoothing plane. I work against a planning stop, holding the workpiece with my hand. Take the first passes slow and use your lower fingers to press the fence against the edge of the board being grooved. After the groove has been started, you can speed up. However, you should still apply pressure to the fence.

Keep the skate running smoothly. Use a shoulder plane to take a few light shavings off the skate, and don't forget to wax the skate before use.

Shopmade Cutting Gauge

BOB VAN DYKE

Accurate joinery is a matter of cutting to a line but not beyond it. So it's necessary to begin with precise layout. One of the best tools for this is a cutting gauge. This precision tool severs the fibers on the surface of the board, creating a clean, deep, and well-defined layout line that is easy to see.

The design I prefer is one by my friend Will Neptune, who made his while a student at North Bennet Street School in Boston. It has a good single-bevel knife for a blade, a large and comfortable fence, and a round beam. The round beam has several benefits. It's easy to see where you are starting and stopping the cut, and the mortise in the gauge's head is drilled rather than chopped, simplifying construction.

Make and mortise the head

Mill a block of hardwood—cherry, tiger maple, and walnut are good choices—to the head's final dimensions. Mill a setup piece to the same dimensions to help dial in machine settings.

It is important to follow this drilling and mortising sequence: Drill a hole to receive the threaded insert. This should be in the exact center of the end of the head blank and about halfway down. Lay out a ⅝-in.-dia. circle on the face, and then a ¼-in.-sq. mortise tangent to the circle. I cut the mortise with a hollow-chisel mortiser. I cut in halfway from both faces, using a

A Shopmade Marking Gauge

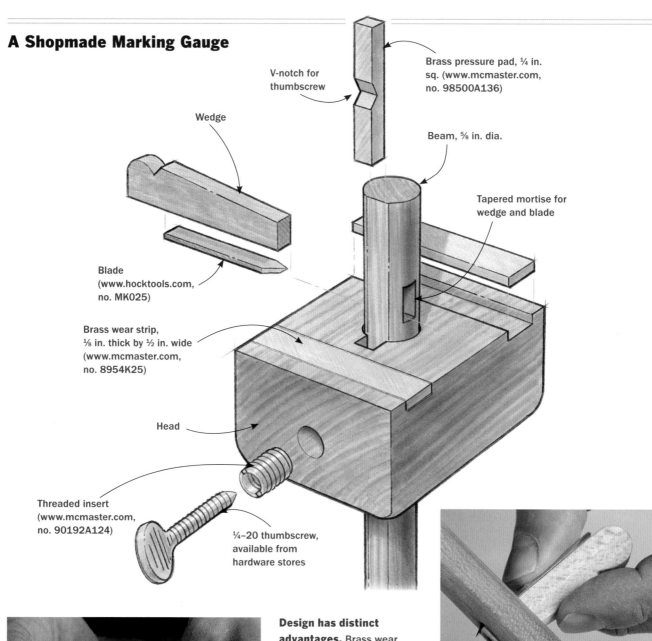

Brass pressure pad, ¼ in. sq. (www.mcmaster.com, no. 98500A136)

V-notch for thumbscrew

Wedge

Beam, ⅝ in. dia.

Tapered mortise for wedge and blade

Blade (www.hocktools.com, no. MK025)

Brass wear strip, ⅛ in. thick by ½ in. wide (www.mcmaster.com, no. 8954K25)

Head

Threaded insert (www.mcmaster.com, no. 90192A124)

¼–20 thumbscrew, available from hardware stores

Design has distinct advantages. Brass wear strips ensure that this gauge will last for years, while the screw and pressure pad lock the beam securely in the mortise so that it doesn't move during use. The round beam lets you see exactly where the point of the blade is, allowing you to start and stop a cut with great precision.

Single-bevel blade is more accurate. The blade in this gauge cuts a deeper, cleaner, more precise line than either the pin of a traditional marking gauge or the round cutter of a wheel gauge. Orient the bevel toward the gauge's head so that it pulls the gauge tight to the workpiece as it cuts.

Make the Head First

The hole for the threaded insert and the mortise for the beam must be square to the surface. After you've cut them and installed the threaded insert, finish off the head by adding brass wear strips and rounding the back edges.

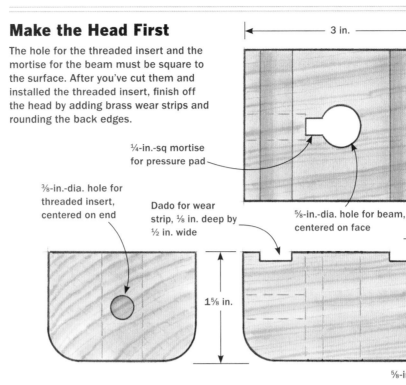

¼-in.-sq mortise for pressure pad

⅜-in.-dia. hole for threaded insert, centered on end

Dado for wear strip, ⅛ in. deep by ½ in. wide

⅝-in.-dia. hole for beam, centered on face

¼ in.

3 in.

2¼ in.

1⅝ in.

⅝-in. radius

Drill for the threaded insert. Centered in one end, the hole extends halfway through the head. To steady the head during drilling, Van Dyke presses it into the corner of a right-angle fence.

Mortise for the pressure pad. To cut the square mortise, go halfway through from one face, flip the head over, and finish the cut. A stop block ensures perfect alignment.

A hole for the beam. Again using the L-shaped fence to steady the head, drill completely through from one side, using a piece of MDF beneath to prevent blowout.

Seat the insert beneath the surface. To ensure that it ends up square to the surface, Van Dyke uses an unplugged drill press to begin threading the insert. The head is held steady in the jaws of a hand screw (right). Then he puts the driver into a ratchet to recess the insert (far right).

Rout dadoes for the wear strips. These should be a bit shallower than the brass strips are thick. Use a fresh backer block to prevent blowout and to steady the small block.

Install the threaded insert now. I use an unplugged drill press to ensure that it goes in straight. Insert the driver bit and turn the chuck by hand while keeping downward pressure on the drill-press handles. I finish recessing the insert with a ratchet (see the bottom photos on p. 199).

Now rout the dadoes for the brass wear strips. Make them shallow enough that the strips sit just proud of the surface. Because these dadoes are routed across the grain, knife the edges of the cuts before running them on the router table. Back up the block so it does not blow out as the bit exits the cut. Glue the brass wear strips into the head with epoxy. After the glue dries, sand the strips flush and remove any squeeze-out. Finally, round over the back side of the head.

stop clamped to the fence to locate the head accurately. Back at the drill press, drill the hole for the beam. Make sure to back up the piece with a fresh piece of plywood or MDF to prevent blowout as the bit exits the hole. For safety and accuracy, use a right-angle fence to support the head.

Round beam makes gauge user-friendly

The gauge's beam begins its life as a ⅝-in.-dia. dowel. Dowels can be inconsistent in diameter, so I knock the dowel through a dowel plate and sand and scrape it to get a tight fit that still slides smoothly.

Epoxy for the brass. Spread a thick layer over the bottom and walls of the dado before setting the brass wear strip into it.

Use a jig to press them in. Dowels, cut in half and glued to a block of hardwood, direct pressure over the strips. Let the glue dry before leveling the strips.

Sand to level the strips. Start with coarse paper and work up 220 grit. Work on a flat surface, like a piece of ¼-in.-thick glass, or the table of a jointer or tablesaw.

Clamp the dowel in a bench vise and plane a flat on one side. The flat should be the same width as the brass key stock you'll use later for the pressure pad.

Now cut the mortise for the blade and wedge. The front end of the mortise is angled about 8°. The back end is perpendicular. I cut the mortise with a hollow-chisel mortiser, holding the dowel in a jig (see the drawing on p. 202). To make the square end of the mortise, hold the dowel in the jig with a wedge underneath. This ensures that the beam is parallel to the mortiser's work table. Remove the wedge to cut the angled front end of the mortise.

To lock the beam in the head and allow for precise adjustments, a thumbscrew presses on a pressure pad made from brass key stock. When tightened, this pad will press against the flat planed into the beam. File a V-shaped groove into the middle of the brass pad and then grind a matching point into the end of

Round over the back edges. Van Dyke uses a ⅝-in.-radius roundover bit and guides the workpiece past the bit using a backer board. Shaping can also be done with hand tools. The key is to make the head comfortable to hold.

Mortise the Beam and Fit the Wedge

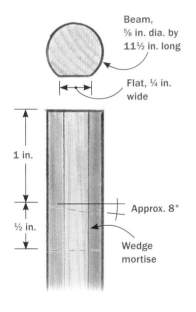

Beam,
⅝ in. dia. by
11½ in. long

Flat, ¼ in. wide

1 in.

½ in.

Approx. 8°

Wedge mortise

Flatten one side. Clamp the beam in a bench vise and carefully plane a flat into it (left). Stop when the flat is as wide as the brass pressure pad (above).

Simple Jig for Mortising

A rabbeted block allows the beam to be clamped securely for mortising. Remove the wedge to cut the second end at an angle.

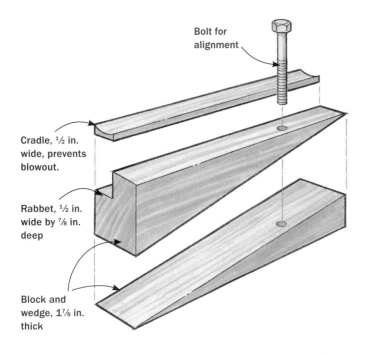

Bolt for alignment

Cradle, ½ in. wide, prevents blowout.

Rabbet, ½ in. wide by ⅞ in. deep

Block and wedge, 1⅞ in. thick

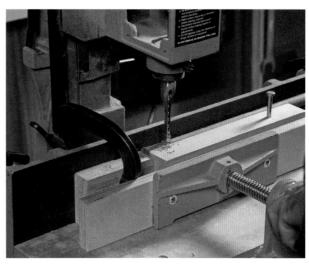

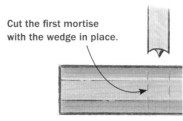

Cut the first mortise with the wedge in place.

Cut the wedge mortise in two steps. Begin with the end closest to the head, which is cut with the beam parallel to the mortiser's bed (above). Remove the wedge to cut the opposite end of the mortise at an angle to match the wedge that secures the blade in the mortise (left).

2⅝ in.

1½ in.

9¾ in.

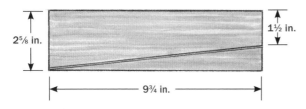

Flat on beam registers against mortiser fence.

Gap between fence and jig puts all clamping pressure on the beam.

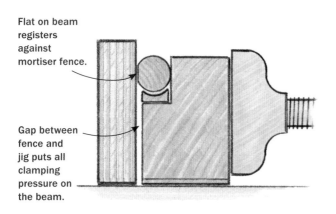

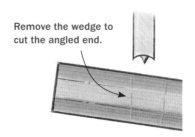

Remove the wedge to cut the angled end.

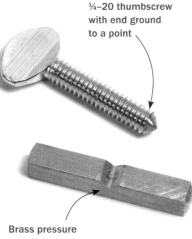

¼–20 thumbscrew with end ground to a point

Brass pressure pad, ¼ in. sq. by 1⅝ in. long, with V-notch

Notch the pressure pad and grind the thumbscrew to fit. File a V-notch in the brass bar stock (above). Then use a guide block to grind the thumbscrew (right). Angled 45° to the sanding belt, it helps create a point that fits into the V-notch.

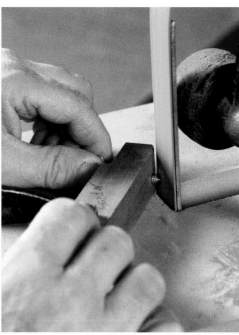

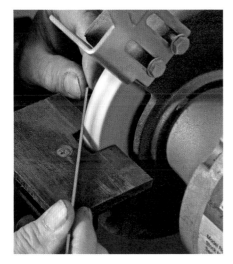

The blade is easy. Van Dyke uses a ¼-in. marking knife from Hock Tools for the gauge's blade, cutting off the first 2 in. at the grinder.

Make the wedge. A simple jig, which holds the blank at the correct angle, ensures the wedge has the same angle as the mortise in the beam.

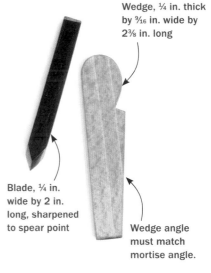

Wedge, ¼ in. thick by 9⁄16 in. wide by 2⅜ in. long

Blade, ¼ in. wide by 2 in. long, sharpened to spear point

Wedge angle must match mortise angle.

the thumbscrew. The groove and matching point hold the pad in place when the screw is loosened.

Now turn your attention to the wedge and cutter. Make the wedge from a tight-grained hardwood. The blank should slide freely in the mortise, and its angle should match the mortise's angle. You can use the wedge from the mortising jig to get this angle.

The gauge needs a good blade, and the best I have found begins life as a Hock Tools ¼-in. marking knife. I cut about 2 in. off the end and grind that to a shallow spear-point profile. Put the blade in the beam with the bevel facing toward the head and the tip protruding about ⅛ in. Lock it in place with the wedge. The bottom end of the wedge probably will stick out too far. Trace around the wedge, pull it out, and cut it down.

After one or two coats of wax, the gauge is ready for use. Always hold the gauge with your hand wrapped around the head and never around the beam.

Trim for clearance. Scribe around the wedge, and then cut it so that it's just proud of the beam. This leaves enough sticking out for you to press the wedge out of the mortise and pull the blade out for sharpening.

4 Bench Jigs for Handplanes

NORMAN PIROLLO

Like many woodworkers, I began with hand tools but quickly progressed to using machines for almost every aspect of my work. A few years ago, as I developed my woodworking business, I decided there must be a less dusty and more peaceful way to make furniture. I took courses at a woodworking school whose philosophy was all about hand tools. This experience opened my eyes; you might say I became a born-again woodworker. Safety was also a factor in my transformation. For example, it can be dangerous to machine small parts on a tablesaw or bandsaw.

Now, instead of hearing the drone and whine of machines and breathing dust all day, I listen to classical music and sweep up shavings at the end of the day.

While I do use machinery sparingly, productivity remains the key to any business, so I've had to make my handplaning efficient without sacrificing quality. I use a series of jigs for different planing situations. The jigs have ¾-in.-dia. dowels that fit into dog holes in my workbench. If your bench doesn't have dog holes already, you need to drill only two or three because all the jigs are interchangeable. The jigs and techniques I'll describe are by no means new—handplanes have been used for centuries—but I've added my own modifications. One of these is that I'm left-handed, so you'll need to flip the plans if you're a righty.

Use a Stop to Go Faster

Aside from efficiency, you get a better feel for the work when the board is held against a single plane stop rather than being pinched between two dogs.

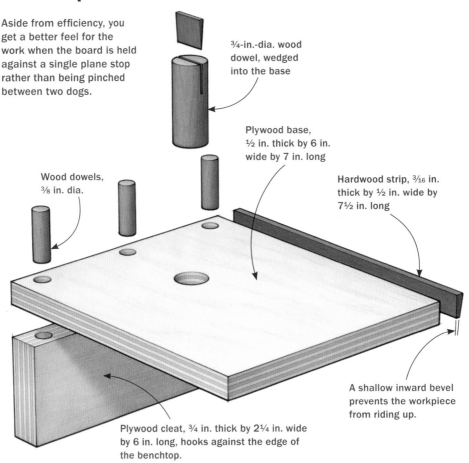

¾-in.-dia. wood dowel, wedged into the base

Plywood base, ½ in. thick by 6 in. wide by 7 in. long

Wood dowels, ⅜ in. dia.

Hardwood strip, ³⁄₁₆ in. thick by ½ in. wide by 7½ in. long

A shallow inward bevel prevents the workpiece from riding up.

Plywood cleat, ¾ in. thick by 2¼ in. wide by 6 in. long, hooks against the edge of the benchtop.

1 Planing stop

For face-planing boards at least ½ in. thick, I use a simple stop that is attached to the bench with a single dowel. To prevent the jig from pivoting in use, a cleat registers against the front edge of the bench.

After cutting out the two parts, clamp them together and place them on the workbench, centered over a dog hole. Insert a ¾-in.-dia. Forstner bit into the hole from the underside of the bench and use the spur to mark the location on the bottom of the jig base. Use the same bit to drill the hole on the drill press, and then use a ⅜-in.-dia. brad-

Locate the big dowel. Center the base over a dog hole. Use a ¾-in. Forstner bit to nick the underside of the base where you will drill.

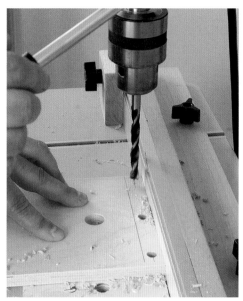

Drill for the others. With a ⅜-in. brad-point bit, drill three holes at the front of the base for dowels that connect the cleat.

point bit to drill three holes for the dowels that will connect the cleat.

Dowel stock varies fractionally in diameter; a slightly loose fit is fine in the dog hole, but you need a tight fit into the base of the jig. To ensure a good fit, I saw a kerf into the top of the ¾-in. dowel. I apply glue and insert the dowel, then compress a hardwood wedge into the kerf using the jaws of a vise, which locks the dowel in place.

When the glue is dry, insert the base into the dog hole, clamp on the cleat, square the base to the edge of the bench, and extend the ⅜-in.-dia. holes into the cleat. Glue in the dowels and, when dry, plane everything flush with the base.

On the working edge of the stop, I glue a strip of hardwood with a shallow inward bevel on its face to keep boards from slipping upward. I apply a single coat of oil finish to my jigs for looks and protection, but this is optional.

2 Bird's-mouth stop

When edge-planing long boards, I employ a bird's-mouth stop. This attachment works remarkably well for holding a board on edge

Attach the cleat. Insert the big dowel, ensure the base is square to the bench, then clamp on the cleat and extend the ⅜-in. dowel holes.

and is much faster than using a front vise, with or without a board jack.

Attached to the bench via two adjacent dog holes, this jig takes a bit more time to make than the last one, but the top two dowels give great rigidity and eliminate

Wedges Hold Long Boards on Edge

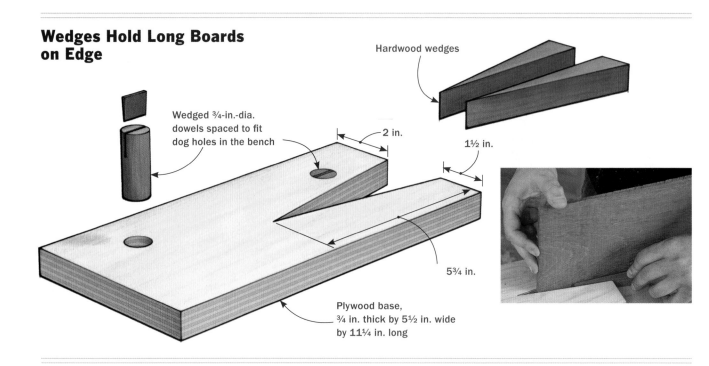

Hardwood wedges

Wedged ¾-in.-dia. dowels spaced to fit dog holes in the bench

2 in.

1½ in.

5¾ in.

Plywood base, ¾ in. thick by 5½ in. wide by 11¼ in. long

Edge-planing made easy. A bird's-mouth jig allows you to rest the whole length of a board on the bench while you edge-plane it. If held in a vise, only a part of the board is supported.

any tendency for rotation. Any board up to about 1½ in. thick can be inserted into the V-shaped slot in the jig and held in place with a small hardwood wedge on either side. The easiest way to make the wedges is to use the opening in the base as a template, cut the wedges on the bandsaw, and then clean them up with a handplane while holding them in a vise.

3 Planing board

I reach for my planing board when working shorter or otherwise difficult workpieces. It combines a flat base with smaller versions of the first two jigs in this chapter.

The planing board has two advantages. It guarantees a flat surface to plane on, even if the benchtop isn't flat. Also, it allows me to plane thin, narrow stock. I add a base of ⅛-in. thick Masonite® to plane stock less than ¼ in. thick instead of installing a thinner plane stop.

If I need to skew the plane slightly to lower the cutting angle and slice through difficult grain, I add a removable side stop that plugs into the planing board using two ½-in.-dia. dowels. This provides lateral support.

For jointing the edges of boards, I attach a smaller version of the bird's-mouth stop. In this way I can plane the face and the edge grain of a short workpiece without removing the planing board.

A flat surface. Even if your benchtop isn't flat, the plywood base of the planing board provides a flat surface to plane on.

The Planing Board Is a Multifunctional Jig

Once you build this planing board, it is likely to become a permanent part of your bench.

Thin stock, no problem. When planing stock less than ¼ in. thick, add an auxiliary base of ⅛-in.-thick Masonite so the plane will clear the stop.

Wedged ¾-in.-dia. dowels spaced to fit alternate benchdog holes

Opening is 1½ in. wide by 5¾ in. deep.

Bird's-mouth stop, plywood, ½ in. thick by 4½ in. wide by 8½ in. long

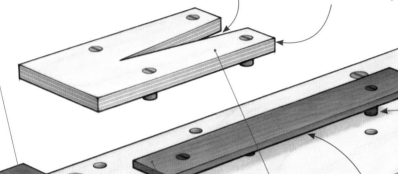

Wedged ½-in.-dia. dowels fit holes in the planing board.

Hardwood side stop, ¼ in. thick by 2 in. wide by 13 in. long

Plywood base, ¾ in. thick by 9 in. wide by 36 in. long

Plane stop, ¼-in.-thick by 2¾-in.-wide by 9-in.-long hardwood, glued to the base

Side support. When you need to skew the plane or plane across the board, use the side stop to support the workpiece laterally.

There's more. Once you've planed the face of the board, use the bird's-mouth attachment to plane the board's edge.

4 Shooting board

When it comes to trimming the ends of boards, especially small ones, I turn to my shooting board. The jig, which hooks over the edge of the benchtop, consists of a base, a fence, and a runway for a handplane to glide along. The plane removes shavings in fine increments, leaving the board the correct length and the ends square and smooth, ready to be used in joinery.

The two-part fence, which supports the work and prevents tearout, must be exactly 90° to the runway and flush with the edge of the top base. The main fence is glued and screwed to the base, while the front face is screwed to the main fence so that it can be shimmed if needed. The best plane to use is a

Square and true. Place the board against the fence with the end fractionally beyond the end of the fence. Slide the plane past it, taking thin shavings until the end of the board is clean and perfectly square.

Basic Shooting Board Planes Ends Square

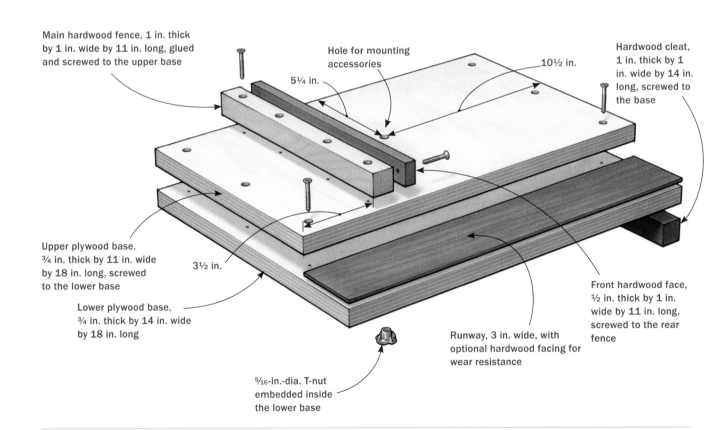

Main hardwood fence, 1 in. thick by 1 in. wide by 11 in. long, glued and screwed to the upper base

Hole for mounting accessories

5¼ in.

10½ in.

Hardwood cleat, 1 in. thick by 1 in. wide by 14 in. long, screwed to the base

Upper plywood base, ¾ in. thick by 11 in. wide by 18 in. long, screwed to the lower base

3½ in.

Lower plywood base, ¾ in. thick by 14 in. wide by 18 in. long

Front hardwood face, ½ in. thick by 1 in. wide by 11 in. long, screwed to the rear fence

Runway, 3 in. wide, with optional hardwood facing for wear resistance

⁵⁄₁₆-in.-dia. T-nut embedded inside the lower base

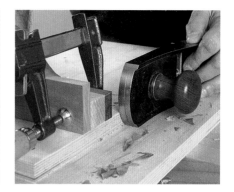

Make a runway for the plane. The 3-in.-wide runway is formed by screwing the upper base to the lower base.

A square fence is critical. If the front face of the fence isn't 90° to the runway, you can shim it.

Trim the end. Before use, trim the fence flush with the edge of the top base. Clamp a piece of scrap to the fence to prevent tearout.

Frame Miters

By adding a 45° plywood fence, you can use the shooting board to fine-tune parts for a mitered frame.

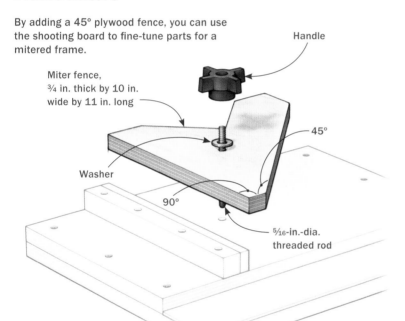

Handle

Miter fence, ¾ in. thick by 10 in. wide by 11 in. long

Washer

45°

90°

⁵⁄₁₆-in.-dia. threaded rod

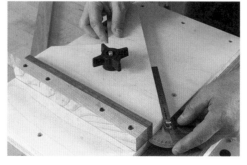

Locate the hole from underneath. Hold the miter fence in position on the shooting board.

Check the angle. Make sure the fence is exactly 45° to the edge of the runway.

Carcase Miters

A second auxiliary fence allows you to trim carcase miters, leaving them at precisely 45° and free of sawmarks.

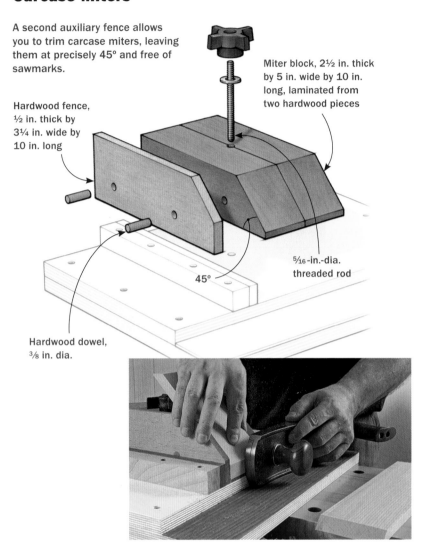

Hardwood fence, ½ in. thick by 3¼ in. wide by 10 in. long

Miter block, 2½ in. thick by 5 in. wide by 10 in. long, laminated from two hardwood pieces

⁵⁄₁₆-in.-dia. threaded rod

45°

Hardwood dowel, ⅜ in. dia.

Laminated block. The large glue surface needs plenty of clamps to create enough pressure.

Quick change. The T-nut, threaded rod, and knob allow quick removal of both miter fences.

low-angle jack plane whose 37° cutting angle, long body, and large mass make it ideal for shaving end grain. Push the plane downward and toward the end of the workpiece with one hand, and use the other to secure the workpiece against the fence. This movement takes a little getting used to but soon becomes second nature.

Two accessories for perfect miters

I recommend two easily installed attachments for this shooting board. The first is a triangular-shaped piece of plywood used to tune a flat, or frame, miter; the second is a larger block of wood with a face angled at 45°, used to trim a standing, or carcase, miter. Both attachments are held to the base using threaded rod that is screwed into a T-nut embedded in the underside of the jig. This group of easily constructed jigs leaves joints that surpass those left by a machine, and does it quicker.

Hand-Built Home for Hand Tools

ANDREW HUNTER

Japanese carpenters are renowned for the sophistication of their wooden joinery, yet they typically build toolboxes of the simplest sort. A traditional Japanese toolbox, butt-joined or dadoed and nailed together, speaks of utility and practicality. It is durable, stackable, and eminently portable.

Although I favor utilitarian toolboxes, I relate to the impulse to make a special project out of creating a home for beloved tools—that's why I build my boxes with hand tools. I still look with pride at the resaw marks on the underside of the lid on my original toolbox, made when I was just starting out and absorbing all I could from Toshio Odate's book, *Japanese Woodworking Tools: Their Tradition, Spirit and Use* (The Taunton Press, 1984). I used Odate's toolbox as a model for my own. The sliding lid provides a strong, satisfying closure and, when removed, is a convenient place to lay out tools for the work at hand. And the inset ends of the box make for stronger joints while also providing handholds.

As I've built more boxes over the years—for toys as well as tools—I've stuck with the original design. I've been tempted to add some furniture-level joinery, but my original nailed toolboxes, going on 15 years old now, are holding up fine, and I really like the way they look, so I've stayed with the traditional nailed joints.

Strong and Simple

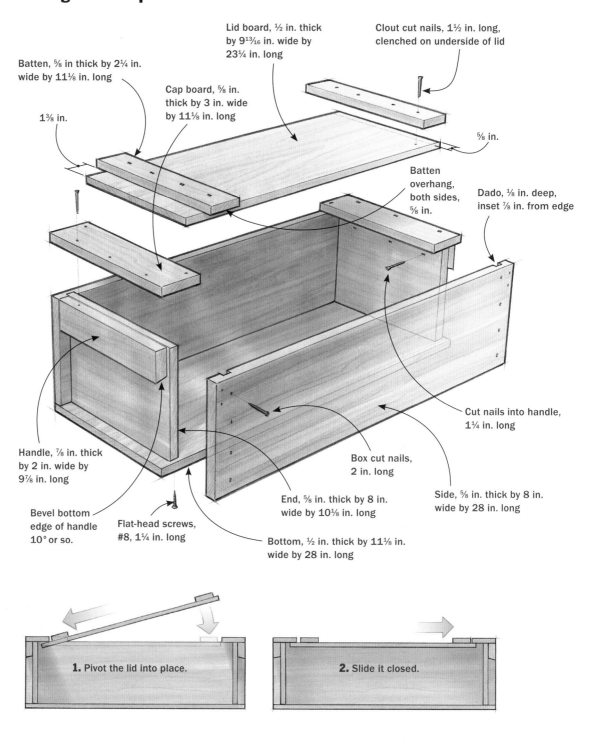

Lid board, ½ in. thick by 9¹³⁄₁₆ in. wide by 23¼ in. long

Clout cut nails, 1½ in. long, clenched on underside of lid

Batten, ⅝ in thick by 2¼ in. wide by 11⅛ in. long

Cap board, ⅝ in. thick by 3 in. wide by 11⅛ in. long

1⅜ in.

⅝ in.

Batten overhang, both sides, ⅝ in.

Dado, ⅛ in. deep, inset ⅞ in. from edge

Handle, ⅞ in. thick by 2 in. wide by 9⅞ in. long

Bevel bottom edge of handle 10° or so.

Flat-head screws, #8, 1¼ in. long

End, ⅝ in. thick by 8 in. wide by 10⅛ in. long

Box cut nails, 2 in. long

Cut nails into handle, 1¼ in. long

Side, ⅝ in. thick by 8 in. wide by 28 in. long

Bottom, ½ in. thick by 11⅛ in. wide by 28 in. long

1. Pivot the lid into place.

2. Slide it closed.

Lay out and cut out. Hunter rough-cut all the parts but the handles from a 12-ft.-long white pine 1x12.

Flatten, then thickness. You can flatten and thickness the parts by hand, as Hunter does, or by machine.

Clean up and crosscut. After thicknessing the sides and jointing their edges, saw the ends square and true the cut with a handplane.

Produce the parts

I built my latest box with a 12-ft.-long 1x12 of white pine—and a thicker scrap for the handles. Although the 1x12 came from my hardware store milled ¾ in. thick, it was far from true, so it required jointing and thicknessing. That was fine, because even in my largest boxes, I find that parts a full ¾ in. thick look chunky. As with other projects in white pine, I gave this box a handplaned surface and left the wood untreated, letting it acquire a patina over time.

Before any cuts are made, lay out the parts on the board, starting with the large pieces. Because the box has cross-grain construction, I try to find pieces for the top and bottom that are largely quartersawn. I also save the outer, clear, radial sections of the board for narrower parts like the lid battens.

Next rough-cut the parts and mill them to thickness. To see how I do this by hand, check out "Prep Rough Lumber with Hand Tools" (p. 152). With the parts milled, cut the sides and ends to size. From there, cut parts as needed during the project, taking measurements directly from the box.

Cut the dadoes

With the sides and end pieces ready, locate the dadoes in the sides that will receive the

Cut the joinery. Use the handle board (above) to determine how far to inset the dado from the end of the side. Then lay out the dado's width directly from the mating end board (right).

Saw the shoulders. Hunter uses a Japanese panel saw guided by a fence to cut the dado shoulders. A line he marked on the sawblade governs the depth of cut.

Get the meat out of the middle. A bench chisel wielded bevel-down removes the waste between the dado shoulders. To refine the cut, Hunter will use a paring action with the chisel held bevel up and parallel to the benchtop.

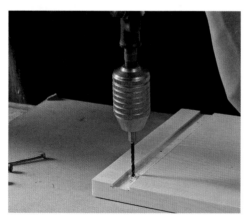

Cut nails get pilot holes. Predrill for the nails using a bit whose diameter matches the thickness (not the full taper) of the cut nails.

end boards. The amount the dado is inset from the end of the side board is determined by the thickness of the handle. Mark this distance and then, with all the parts labeled, use the end boards to lay out the width of their mating dadoes.

I use a Japanese panel saw, or azebiki, to cut the kerfs that define the dado. Clear the waste between the kerfs with a chisel or a specialty plane. Now you're ready to nail the sides together.

Nails and screws

Predrill for the nails, choosing a bit sized to the thickness of the cut nails (not to their width, which tapers), and drill only through the piece the nail enters first. To help align and stabilize the parts while nailing, clamp the box to the bottom board. The bottom will still be oversize at this point, but it should have one long edge jointed and one end cut square. Once the sides and ends of the box are nailed, you can mark the final length and width of the bottom from the box.

The bottom of the box is simply screwed to the sides. This is not only the simplest solution, but I believe it is also the most

Careful with the cut nails. To prevent splitting the top board, turn the cut nail so its taper lines up with the long grain.

durable. There are no fragile edges as with a bottom that is let into a rabbet or a groove. Like an applied back in a cabinet, the bottom of this box offers support against racking, and using screws gives me confidence that the bottom will not be pushed off under a heavy load. Building this way does raise the issue of restricting seasonal movement, but using white pine, a very stable wood, and quartersawn white pine at that, I have had no problems with the boxes I have made in the past.

The bottom squares up the box. After jointing one long edge of the bottom and cutting one end of it square, clamp it in place to help align the box parts for nailing.

Add the bottom. After trimming the bottom board flush to the outside of the box, drill clearance holes and countersinks, and attach it with screws.

Create the top

The lid is one of my favorite things about this box. To close it, you tip the long tongue of the lid under either cap board, lower the lid, and then slide it so the short tongue presses under the opposite cap board. It's a snug fit, and no locking mechanism is needed to keep the lid firmly closed.

Before dimensioning the top, I fit the handles. You can bevel their bottom edge to make the grip more positive. Nail into these parts from the inside of the box and through the sides. You'll also be nailing into them through the cap board; this multidirectional nailing brings real rigidity.

The handle gets a bevel. To make the grip more positive when you lift the box, bevel the bottom edge of the handle at 10° or so.

Secure the handle. After beveling the handle, cut it to length so it's a press-fit between the sides. Then nail it in with short nails from inside the box (left) and longer ones into the end grain from outside (above).

Next, nail the two cap boards that retain the lid at the ends of the top. To avoid the splitting that can occur when nailing close to the end of a board, leave them long until they are nailed in place. Then trim them flush with the sides.

Now it's time to plane the lid board to width. Leave enough of a gap on both sides to accommodate seasonal movement. To determine the final length of the lid board, add 1¼ in. to the distance between the cap boards. This extra length is for the two tongues beyond the cleats that hold the lid shut.

The cleats that keep the lid flat and hold it in position are next. Cut them to length and clench-nail them to the lid board. This simple solution is much stronger than just nailing. Place a sacrificial board on your bench and drive each nail through the cleat and the lid so the nails extend an extra ⅜ in. or so. After prying the lid assembly off the sacrificial board, clench over the end of the nails. This will suck the two pieces together. Finally, chamfer any edges that need it and fill your new box with tools.

Add the lid. With a sacrificial backer board protecting the bench, drive overlong cut nails through the battens and the lid board (above left). Then, after prying the nailed parts off the backer board, bend the tip of each cut nail (above right). As you clench the nails (right), use an anvil or other rock-solid surface to back up the nail head.

Build a Thoroughbred Shaving Horse

TIM MANNEY

The first woodworking I ever did was on a shaving horse. I had just turned 20, and a 12-year-old sat me down at a shaving horse with a drawknife and taught me how to make a spatula from a piece of red maple firewood. I was hooked. The simple elegance and intuitive feel of the horse and drawknife completely drew me in

as shavings piled up around my feet. Since then I've had the good fortune to spend countless hours on shaving horses and to work extensively with other shaving horse aficionados.

My current horse is the offspring of great horses built by two of my mentors. The base comes from Curtis Buchanan's horse, and the

Shaving Horse

Manney builds his horse of southern yellow pine 2x lumber for strength and economy. His design absorbs the lessons of traditional dumbhead-style horses and improves on them. The clamping pedestal, swing arm, and seat all are easily removed for transport or storage.

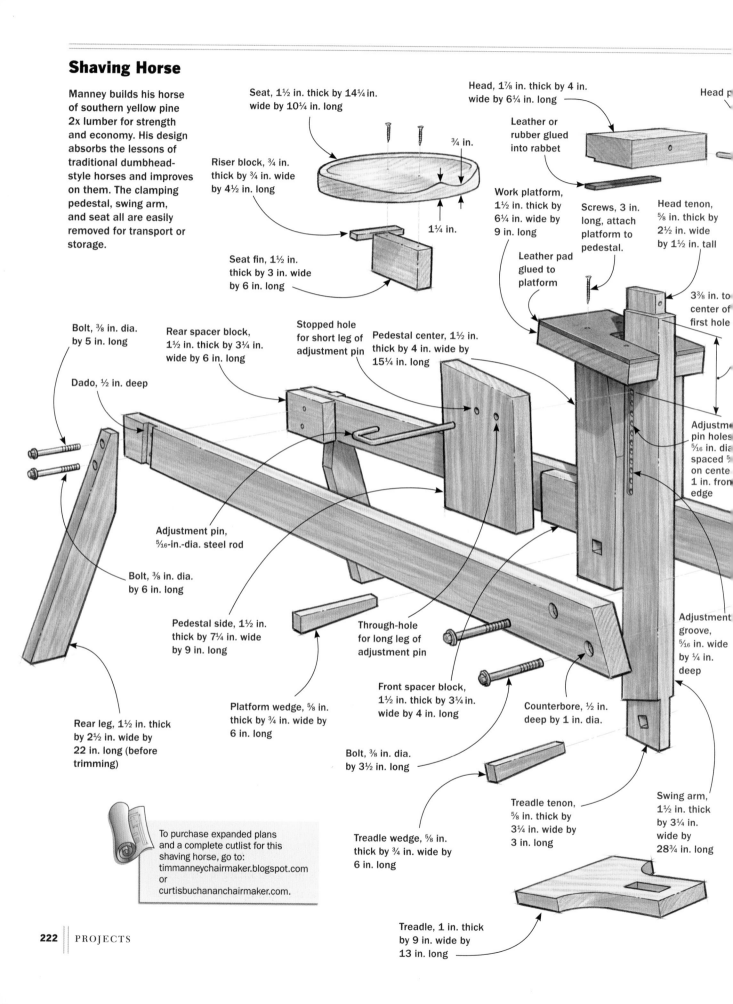

Seat, 1½ in. thick by 14¼ in. wide by 10¼ in. long

Head, 1⅞ in. thick by 4 in. wide by 6¼ in. long

Head p

Riser block, ¾ in. thick by ¾ in. wide by 4½ in. long

¾ in.

1¼ in.

Leather or rubber glued into rabbet

Seat fin, 1½ in. thick by 3 in. wide by 6 in. long

Work platform, 1½ in. thick by 6¼ in. wide by 9 in. long

Screws, 3 in. long, attach platform to pedestal.

Head tenon, ⅝ in. thick by 2½ in. wide by 1½ in. tall

Leather pad glued to platform

3⅜ in. to center of first hole

Bolt, ⅜ in. dia. by 5 in. long

Rear spacer block, 1½ in. thick by 3¼ in. wide by 6 in. long

Stopped hole for short leg of adjustment pin

Pedestal center, 1½ in. thick by 4 in. wide by 15¼ in. long

Dado, ½ in. deep

Adjustme pin holes ⁵⁄₁₆ in. dia spaced on cente 1 in. from edge

Adjustment pin, ⁵⁄₁₆-in.-dia. steel rod

Bolt, ⅜ in. dia. by 6 in. long

Pedestal side, 1½ in. thick by 7¼ in. wide by 9 in. long

Through-hole for long leg of adjustment pin

Adjustment groove, ⁵⁄₁₆ in. wide by ¼ in. deep

Rear leg, 1½ in. thick by 2½ in. wide by 22 in. long (before trimming)

Platform wedge, ⅝ in. thick by ¾ in. wide by 6 in. long

Front spacer block, 1½ in. thick by 3¼ in. wide by 4 in. long

Counterbore, ½ in. deep by 1 in. dia.

Swing arm, 1½ in. thick by 3¼ in. wide by 28¾ in. long

Bolt, ⅜ in. dia. by 3½ in. long

Treadle tenon, ⅝ in. thick by 3¼ in. wide by 3 in. long

Treadle wedge, ⅝ in. thick by ¾ in. wide by 6 in. long

To purchase expanded plans and a complete cutlist for this shaving horse, go to: timmanneychairmaker.blogspot.com or curtisbuchananchairmaker.com.

Treadle, 1 in. thick by 9 in. wide by 13 in. long

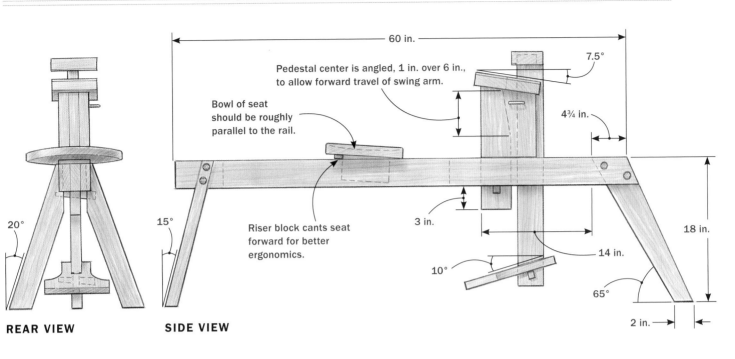

60 in.

Pedestal center is angled, 1 in. over 6 in., to allow forward travel of swing arm.

7.5°

Bowl of seat should be roughly parallel to the rail.

4¾ in.

20°

15°

Riser block cants seat forward for better ergonomics.

3 in.

10°

14 in.

18 in.

65°

2 in.

REAR VIEW

SIDE VIEW

Rail, 1½ in. thick by 3¼ in. wide by 60 in. long

clamping mechanism is a simplified version of Carl Swensson's. By crossbreeding these two steeds I got a strong, simple-to-build shaving horse that adjusts easily for different-size workpieces and has a very powerful grip. It looks similar to traditional dumbhead-style horses, which grip the work with a block-shaped head rather than a clamping bar, but it offers increased holding power and better ergonomics.

Front leg, 1½ in. thick by 4½ in. wide by 20 in. long (before trimming)

For me, the horse starts with a single 16-ft. 2x10 of clear southern yellow pine. With thoughtful layout and a blemish-free plank, this is enough material for the entire horse. In New England, where I live, southern yellow pine can be hard to find. But I discovered that OSHA-approved walkboard planks for scaffolding are made of it, and a good construction-lumber supplier should have them in stock. In the absence of yellow pine, a medium-soft hardwood like tulip poplar would work, or, in the Northwest, clear Douglas fir.

Begin with the beam

The base of a shaving horse needs to be extremely solid. If the base can flex, your horse will creak, moan, and trot across the floor as you work—undesirable traits for a horse of this sort. The laminated-beam construction I use makes for a very rigid base that won't flex under the heaviest use.

To make the beam, start by milling the spacer blocks and the front leg to the same thickness and then gluing the spacer blocks

Base

The spaced double-rail structure of the beam provides rigidity without excess weight and also creates the slot that neatly accepts the front leg, pedestal, swing arm, and seat.

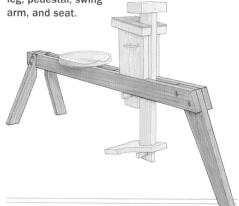

The spine of a horse. Manney creates a stout beam by gluing spacers between a pair of rails. He trims the assembly afterward with a pass through the planer.

Front leg first. Cut from stock milled to the same thickness as the spacers, the front leg is glued in next. When the glue dries, Manney adds carriage bolts to the joint.

between the rails. Wait to glue the front leg in place until after the spacer blocks have cured. This lets you true up the beam by passing it through the planer after the initial glue-up. It also lets you take your time to get the front leg aligned just right at glue-up.

Fit and fix the legs

All three legs should be several inches overlength at assembly; you'll trim them to final length only after they're all glued and

Dadoes in the beam. Multiple kerfs with a circular saw (left) make quick work of roughing out the angled dadoes for the rear legs. Manney follows up with chisels (above) and a router plane.

bolted. The front leg is tapered, being wider at the top to allow for a greater offset between the two bolts that will hold it in place. If the bolts were placed one directly above the other, they would provide much less resistance to racking forces. I glue in the front leg and then drill counterbores and clearance holes for its bolts, nuts, and washers. With those bolts in place, it's on to the rear legs.

The rear legs fit into angled dadoes in the rails of the beam that produce the legs' 15° backward rake. To rough out the dadoes and establish their depth, I cut multiple kerfs with a circular saw. I clear the waste and chop the shoulders with chisels and then clean up the bottom of the dadoes with a router plane. Alternately, you could cut these dadoes with a router. The fit should be tight to prevent the rear legs from racking over time.

Drilling for the bolts through the back legs takes some finessing. Start by drawing a square line across the top of the beam from the center of one dado to the other. Then clamp the legs in position, leaving enough room above the clamps to drill the top hole. I drill the counterbores first, then the bolt-clearance hole. Using the line across the top as a sighting aid, drill the clearance hole with a long 7/16-in. bit, drilling in from both sides. You might want to have a friend—or a mirror—on hand to help ensure that the bit stays horizontal as you drill.

If the bolt slides right through the clearance hole, take a moment to give yourself a little pat on the back. If it doesn't, wallow out the hole with your drill bit, or chase through the original hole with a larger bit to create more clearance. Insert and tighten the upper bolt, then remove the clamps and drill the lower hole. When that's finished, spread glue on the dadoes and bolt the rear legs in place.

With all three legs glued and bolted to the beam, find a large flat surface so you can level

Boring for a bolt. After counterboring for the top bolt, Manney carefully drills the clearance hole.

Flatten the tops. A thin shim protects the beam as Manney saws the rear legs nearly flush.

the legs. The goal, after trimming, is to have the top of the beam 18 in. from the floor. Use blocks and wedges under the legs to get the horse level from side to side and front to back. Then use a scribe—I clamp a pencil to a scrap of wood—to mark a cut line around each leg. If the beam is 21 in. above the flat surface, for example, you'll need a 3-in.-high scribe. Cut to the scribe lines with a handsaw, chamfer the edges with a knife or a chisel, and you've completed the base.

The heart of the horse

The clamping mechanism is the heart and soul of this shaving horse. The tight tolerances of the work platform and the swing arm prevent the head from racking

Shim and trim. After shimming the legs until the beam is parallel with the bench, scribe a line around each leg. Then cut them to length.

and make for a stronger grip. And a simple improvement to the height-adjustment mechanism makes the horse far easier to use. Like many dumbhead-style shaving horses, this one has a row of holes that allow you to adjust the swing arm up and down to accept thick or thin workpieces. But on this horse, the adjustment holes all lie in a groove. As you draw the pin from the hole to adjust the height of the head, the pin remains in the groove, making it simpler to slide the pin into one of the holes above or below.

The pedestal that supports the work platform is laminated from three pieces. The center piece forms a long tenon and has a wedged mortise at the bottom that locks the assembly to the beam. The angle cut on its front edge allows the swing arm to pivot all the way forward. The center piece should be thicknessed so that it just slides between the rails of the beam. The two outer pieces of the pedestal form massive tenon shoulders that pull tight against the rails of the beam when the wedge is driven home.

Pedestal

The clamping pedestal, a U-shaped unit that slots into the beam, is built wide to maximize stability and is held firmly in place by a wedge below.

The pedestal is a sandwich. Having already glued one side of the pedestal to the center board, Manney uses the beam to support and register the work as he glues on the second side.

A slice off the pedestal. After glue-up, cut the top of the pedestal at an 82.5° angle.

Mark for the mortise. Strike a line along the bottom of the beam to locate the mortise for the wedge that will lock the pedestal in place.

Drill and chop. Cut the top cheek of the mortise slightly over the line to be sure the wedge will pull the pedestal fully home.

Platform

The platform serves as the lower jaw of the vise. It is canted upward at 7.5° to improve ergonomics.

Cover the platform. Glue leather to the top face of the work platform (left), then screw the platform to the pedestal, sinking the screws below the surface of the leather (above).

When you glue the side pieces to the center piece, be sure to orient them pith-side in. Flatsawn yellow pine boards this wide will cup a little over time. Placing them this way should prevent them from cupping in toward the swing arm and pinching it.

On to the swing arm

When the work pedestal is glued up and wedged to the base, plane the swing arm to fit the channel in the pedestal. The swing arm should move easily, but it shouldn't be loose—a good fit here will prevent the swing arm from racking to the left or right when a piece of wood is held under only one side of the jaw.

With the swing arm dimensioned, drill the height-adjustment holes and rout the groove they sit in. I drill the holes 1 in. from the front edge of the arm. The groove should be on the same side of the horse as your dominant hand when you are on the horse.

I prefer a low-profile head on the shaving horse. That makes it easier to reach over the head to work on the front side of the swing arm and keeps you from ever having to push the drawknife. The joint that attaches the head to the swing arm is a bit odd. The mortise is oriented across the grain of the head, with end grain forming the two long side walls. This is not ideal for joint strength, but it's the trade-off that lets me keep the

Swing Arm

The swing arm is essentially a long lever that translates foot pressure into gripping power.

Start the treadle tenon. Manney makes most of the cheek cut on the bandsaw, but because the shoulder is angled, he can't complete it there. He finishes the cut with a handsaw.

Piercing the treadle. After drilling out most of the waste. Manney uses chisels to clean up the mortise in the treadle.

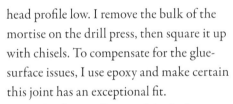

head profile low. I remove the bulk of the mortise on the drill press, then square it up with chisels. To compensate for the glue-surface issues, I use epoxy and make certain this joint has an exceptional fit.

I make the treadle next. I do the layout on a rectangular blank and take it to the drill press to rough out the through-mortise for the swing arm. Next I cut out the overall shape at the bandsaw. You can clean up the sawn edges or leave them as is, as I would tend to do. Last, I clean up the sides and ends of the mortise with chisels.

With the head and treadle made and mortised, I cut the tenons on both ends of the swing arm. Before gluing on the head, I cut a rabbet into its gripping edge and glue in a strip of thick leather or 80A polyurethane rubber. This will make the head grippier and keep it from denting the workpiece. With the jaw lining installed, glue the head to the swing arm. Once the glue has cured and the clamps are off, drill through the tenon, insert a piece of ¼-in. steel rod, and epoxy it in place.

Wedge issue. With the tenon finished, fit the treadle and strike a line to begin mortise layout for the wedge that will hold the treadle in place.

On with the head. Manney glues the head with epoxy because the mortise cheeks are mostly end grain. He uses an angled cutoff as a clamping caul.

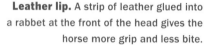

Leather lip. A strip of leather glued into a rabbet at the front of the head gives the horse more grip and less bite.

An important little pin

I bend the end of the adjustment pin to a U-shape, so it's easier to grasp. I insert the short leg in a stopped hole to keep the pin stationary as I work. A propane torch provides plenty of heat for bending the 5/16-in.-dia. rod. Locate the first bend by inserting the pin into the pedestal as far as it will go and making a mark on the pin ½ in. from the surface of the wood. Use an awl so that the mark will not disappear when the rod is heated. Heat the pin, place the mark in line with the jaw of a metal vise, and bend the remaining portion of the rod 90°. Make

Preparing the adjustment pin. Use a propane torch to heat the steel rod and bend it in a vise (above). Once it's bent and cut to size, insert the long leg in the through-hole and mark for a stopped hole (right) for the short leg.

Seat

The seat's fin is a friction fit in the beam, making it easy to move the seat fore and aft to adjust for the size of the workpiece (and the worker).

Scoop and saw. After scooping out the seat with a scorp and a spokeshave, Manney cuts it to shape at the bandsaw.

Fin details. Attach the fin with countersunk screws through the top of the seat (left). Then add a riser block at the back (below) to tip the seat forward for better ergonomics.

a second bend 1½ in. from the first, and cut the short leg to length. Then insert the long leg and use the short leg to locate the position of the stopped hole. Now put the swing arm in place and install the adjustment pin to make sure everything glides smoothly. Sometimes the pin requires some light filing to keep the swing arm from binding.

All the horse lacks now is a seat. The one I like is based on a stool by Pete Galbert. It is big enough to be comfortable, and small enough that you won't bump it getting on and off. After the seat is shaped, I attach a fin to the bottom that fits between the rails of the beam. Then I add a riser block at the back to give it a slight forward tilt. Now this horse is ready to ride.

Saddle up. The seat is a friction fit in the gap between the beam's rails, so it can easily be adjusted up and back for comfort.

Contributors

Christian Becksvoort is a *Fine Woodworking* contributing editor.

Brian Boggs makes chairs in Asheville, N.C.

Tom Calisto is a saw maker and teacher from Apex, N.C.

Dan Faia heads the Cabinet and Furniture Making Program at North Bennet Street School in Boston, Mass.

John Reed Fox is a woodworker and furniture maker in Acton, Mass.

Chris Gochnour is a professional furniture maker and hand-tool expert in Salt Lake City, Nev. (www.chrisgochnour.com).

Garrett Hack, a longtime *Fine Woodworking* contributing editor, is a professional furniture maker in Vermont.

Andrew Hunter designs and builds custom furniture in Accord, N.Y.

Matt Kenney is a senior editor at *Fine Woodworking.*

Philip C. Lowe is a professional furniture maker and the director of The Furniture Institute of Massachusetts.

Tim Manney builds chairs and hand tools in Brunswick, Maine.

Jeff Miller makes custom furniture and teaches woodworking in his Chicago shop. Visit www.furnituremaking.com for more information.

Norman Pirollo is the owner of Refined Edge Furniture Design in Ottawa, Ont., Canada.

Timothy Rousseau, who lives in Appleton, Maine, is a professional furniture maker and instructor at the Center for Furniture Craftsmanship (www.woodschool.org).

Matthew Teague is a furniture maker and writer based in Nashville, Tenn.

Vic Tesolin enjoys building furniture with hand tools in his well-insulated shop outside of Ottawa, Ont., Canada.

Bob Van Dyke is the founder and director of the Connecticut Valley School of Woodworking in Manchester, Conn.

Credits

All photos are courtesy of *Fine Woodworking* magazine, © The Taunton Press, Inc., except as noted below.

Front and Back Cover: Shutterstock

The articles in this book appeared in the following issues of *Fine Woodworking*:

pp. 5–11: Essential Hand-Tool Kit by Dan Faia, issue 251. Photos by Asa Christiana.

pp. 12–19: Combo Squares: The Basics and Beyond by Timothy Rousseau, issue 259. Photos by Matthew Kenney.

pp. 20–23: Every Woodworker Needs a Cutting Gauge by Timothy Rousseau, issue 246. Photos by Matthew Kenney.

pp. 24–29: Machinist's Calipers by Timothy Rousseau, issue 247. Photos by *Fine Woodworking* staff. Drawings by John Tetrault.

pp. 30–35: Mastering the Card Scraper by Matthew Teague, issue 201. Photos by *Fine Woodworking* staff. Drawings by *Fine Woodworking* staff.

pp. 36–39: You Need a Cabinet Scraper by Philip C. Lowe, issue 234. Photos by Matthew Kenney. Drawings by John Tetrault.

pp. 40–47: 4 Planes for Joinery by Vic Tesolin, issue 246. Photos by Matthew Kenney. Drawings by Vince Babak.

pp. 48–57: Get to Know Japanese Handplanes by Andrew Hunter, issue 260. Photos by Anissa Kapsales. Drawings by Vince Babak.

pp. 58–63: Turn Your Shoulder Plane into a Star Performer by Philip C. Lowe, issue 226. Photos by Matthew Kenney.

pp. 64–66: Got a Skew Chisel? by Garrett Hack, issue 217. Photos by Tom McKenna. Drawings by John Tetrault.

pp. 67–73: Choosing and Using Japanese Chisels by John Reed Fox, issue 233. Photos by Mike Pekovich. Drawings by John Hartman.

pp. 74–79: Setting Up Your New Japanese Chisel by John Reed Fox, issue 233. Photos by Mike Pekovich.

pp. 80–83: 4 Must-Have Handsaws by Matthew Kenney, issue 231. Photos by Mike Pekovich.

pp. 84–90: Get Sharp the Diamond Way by Brian Boggs, issue 242. Photos by John Tetrault and Jon Binzen.

pp. 92–97: Skill-Building Hand-Tool Exercises by Jeff Miller, issue 239. Photos by Steve Scott except for p. 92 by John Tetrault.

p. 98–103: Do More with Your Block Plane by Jeff Miller, issue 241. Photos by Asa Christiana.

pp. 104–107: Three Ways to Clamp a Drawer for Planing by Matthew Kenney, issue 238. Photos by Matthew Kenney. Drawings by Vince Babak.

pp. 108–115: Saw Like an Old Pro by Chris Gochnour, issue 235. Photos by Matthew Kenney. Drawings by John Tetrault.

pp. 116–121: 4 Chisel Tricks by Philip C. Lowe, issue 221. Photos by Matthew Kenney.

pp. 122–124: File Joints for a Perfect Fit by Chris Gochnour, issue 247. Photos by Matthew Kenney.

pp. 125–130: Smooth Curves with Hand Tools by Jeff Miller, issue 234. Photos on pp. 125-126 by *Fine Woodworking* staff except for p. 126 by Mario Rodriguez (chest), p. 126 by Skylar Nielson (desk), and p. 126 by Tanya Tucka (chair). Photos on pp. 127-130 by Steve Scott. Drawings by Kelly Dunton.

pp. 131–138: Make the Spokeshave Your Secret Weapon by Chris Gochnour, issue 245. Photos by Ben Blackmar. Drawings by Kelly Dunton.

pp. 139–145: Create Your Own Scratch Stocks by Garrett Hack, issue 254. Photos by Tom McKenna. Drawings by *Fine Woodworking* staff.

pp. 146–151: Make Custom Moldings by Garrett Hack, issue 243. Photos by Matthew Kenney. Drawings by John Tetrault.

pp. 152–157: Prep Rough Lumber with Hand Tools by Andrew Hunter, issue 239. Photos by Jon Binzen. Drawings by Kelly Dunton.

pp. 158–173: Don't Fear the Hand-Cut Dovetail by Christian Becksvoort, issue 238. Photos by Jon Binzen. Drawings by Kelly Dunton.

pp. 175–185: Build Your Own Handsaw by Tom Calisto, issue Tools & Shops winter 2017. Photos by Dillon Ryan except for p. 175 by John Tetrault. Drawings by John Tetrault.

pp. 186–190: Custom Scrapers for Custom Work by Garrett Hack, issue 259. Photos by Tom McKenna. Drawings by John Tetrault.

pp. 191–196: Make a Pair of Grooving Planes by Matthew Kenney, issue 219. Photos by Anissa Kapsales and Kelly Dunton. Drawings by Kelly Dunton.

pp. 197–204: Shopmade Cutting Gauge by Bob Van Dyke, issue 261. Photos by Matthew Kenney. Drawings by Dan Thornton.

pp. 205–212: 4 Bench Jigs for Handplanes by Norman Pirollo, issue 202. Photos by Mark Schofield except for p. 207 (top left) by Norman Pirollo. Drawings by Christopher Mills.

pp. 213–220: Hand-Built Home for Hand Tools by Andrew Hunter, issue 257. Photos by Jon Binzen. Drawings by Dan Thornton.

pp. 221–231: Build a Thoroughbred Shaving Horse by Tim Manney, issue 262. Photos by Jon Binzen. Drawings by Dan Thornton.

Index

Note: Page numbers in *italics* indicate projects.

A
Awls, 7, 230

B
Backsaws, 81, 108–09, 177
Bevel gauge, 6, 17, 52
Bevels, block planes for, 101–02
Bird's-mouth stop, *207–08*
Block planes, 98–103
  advantages of, 98
  angle of blade, 98
  for curves, 127 (*see also* Moldings, custom (making))
  how to push/pull, 98–99, 100–101
  keeping blade sharp, 98
  tips for using/maintaining, 98–99
  uses/using, 99–103
Boards, rough, prepping, 153–57
Burnishers/burnishing, 8, 33, 38

C
Cabinet scrapers, 8, 36–39
Cabriole legs, 120–21, 137, 138
Calipers, 24–29
Carcase miter jig, *212*
Carcase saw, 8, 9, 108, 175–85
Card scrapers, 8, 30–35, 127, 186–89
Case joinery, rabbet planes for, 44–46
Chamfering, 101–02, 117, 179–81, 195
Chisels
  1-in. paring chisel, 9
  set of, 9
  setting bevel angle, 65–66
  skew chisel, 64–66
Chisels, using
  angling to control chopping cuts, 118–19
  chamfering, 117
  for concave curves, 120–21
  cutting layout lines for precise paring, 117–18
  paring to a line, 96–97
  skill-building exercises, 96–97
  slicing off dowels, 97

squaring up holes, 97
  tricks for, 116–21
Clamping drawers for planing, 104–07
Combination squares, 13–19
  checking plane body with, 59–60
  gripping, 16–19
  illustrated, 6
  new, checking, 13
  sizes, 14
  uses/using, 5–6, 13–19
Compass planes, 126
Compasses, 7
Coping saws, 8–9, 82–83
Crosscut saws, 81–82
Curves
  block planes for, 127 (*see also* Moldings, custom (making))
  chisels for, 120–21
  compass plane for, 126
  concave, 120–21, 129, 133–34, 135, 136, 150–51
  convex, 96, 102, 120–21, 126, 127, 128, 134, 135 (*see also* Moldings, custom (making))
  handplanes for, 126–27
  rasps for, 127, 130
  smooth, tools/tips for, 125–30
  spokeshaves for, 125, 127, 128–29, 131–37
  styles of, 126
Cutting gauge, about/using, 20–23
Cutting gauge, making, *197–204*
  drawings for, 198, 199
  making, mortising head, 197–200
  mortising beam, 201–02
  user-friendly round beam, 200–204

D
Diamond stones and paste. *See* Sharpening, diamond for
Dividers, 7
Dovetail saws
  illustrated, 8
  making. *See* Saws, building your own handsaw
  uses/using, 8, 81
Dovetails, 158–73
  about: overview of making, 158–60

anatomy of through-dovetail, 159
block planes for, 100
chopping between tails, 164–67
combination squares for, 17–19
filing for perfect fit, 122–24
gap fixes, 172–73
gluing up, 171
layout, 162–63
mapping out tails and pins, 160–61
paring pins to fit joints, 170–71
pins vs. tails, 158–60
removing waste between pins, 168–70
sawing, 111, 161, 162, 163–64
skew chisel for, 64–66
transferring tails precisely, 167–68
Dowels, slicing off, 97
Dozuki saws, 82
Drawers
  clamping for planing, 104–07
  dovetails for. *See* Dovetails
  leveling edges of, 100–101
Drawknives, 10, 11, 221, 228

E
Edge-banding, trimming, 99
Edges
  easing, 101–02
  profiling/rounding, 136, 137
  shooting on the bench, 157

F
Files
  choosing, 122
  half-round, 11
  mill, 11, 31, 32, 122, 140
  for perfect joint fits, 122–24
  rasps, 10–11, 127, 130, 178–80, 181
Frame miter jig, *211, 212*

G
Grooving planes, making pair of, *191–96*
  about: overview of, 191
  adding core, 193
  body construction, 191–92
  finishing touches, 195–96

making/fitting we[...] 192–95
starting with blades, 19[...]
using planes after, 196

H
Half-round files, 11
Handplanes. *See also* Block planes; Japanese handplanes
  about: overview of types/uses, 7
  bench jigs for. *See* Handplanes, jigs for
  compass plane, 126
  for curves, 126–27
  illustrated, 7
  making pair of grooving planes, 191–96
  planing convex curves, 96
  plow plane, 46–47
  prepping rough lumber, 153–57
  rabbet plane, 44–46, 150
  router plane, 10, 42–44
  shoulder plane, 10, 40–42, 58–63, 196
  skill-building exercises, 95–96
  square shaving with, 61–63
  tips for using, 95–96 (*see also* Block planes)
  using on drawers. *See* Drawers
Handplanes, jigs for, *205–12*
  about: overview of, 205
  bird's-mouth stop, *207–08*
  multifunctional planing board, *208–09*
  planing stop, *206–07*
  shooting board (with frame and carcase miters), *210–12*
Hinges, mortising, 11, 42, 43, 70, 118–19

J
Japanese chisels
  about: overview of, 67–68
  anatomy of, illustrated, 68
  back of blade, 68–69
  benefits of, 67–68
  choosing, 70–73
  oiling, preventing rust, 77
  prices, 72–73
  profiles and finishes, illustrated, 69